D1462060

THE HISTORY OF
SMITH & WESSON FIREARMS

DEAN K. BOORMAN

THE HISTORY OF
SMITH & WESSON FIREARMS

DEAN K. BOORMAN

THE LYONS PRESS

A Salamander Book

Published in the United States by The Lyons Press
Guilford, CT 06437
www.lyonspress.com
An imprint of The Globe Pequot Press

© Salamander Books Ltd., 2002

A member of **Chrysalis** Books plc

ISBN 1-58574-721-1

1 2 3 4 5 6 7 8 9 10

All rights reserved. No part of this publication
may be reproduced, stored in a retrieval system or
transmitted in any form or by any means,
electronic, mechanical, photocopying, recording
or otherwise, without the prior permission of
Salamander Books Ltd.

All correspondence concerning the content of
this volume should be addressed to Salamander
Books Ltd.

The Author

Dean K. Boorman is President of the Armor and
Arms Club of New York, formed in 1921,
believed to be the oldest club of collectors in the
western hemisphere, and affiliated to the New
York Metropolitan Museum of Art. He is also a
member of the prestigious American Society of
Arms Collectors, and has written for both the
American Society and the Armor and Arms Club
of New York. He has also written companion
volumes to this book, *The History of Colt Firearms*
and *The History of Winchester Firearms*.

Credits

Project Manager: Ray Bonds
Designers: Twelveotwo
Picture research: Anne Lang
Production: Ian Hughes
Color reproduction: Anorax Imaging Ltd
Printed and bound in Taiwan

Publisher's Note

This is not an official publication. It is recognized that some words, model names, and designations mentioned herein are the property of the trademark holder. They have been used here for identification purposes only.

Acknowledgments

The publishers wish to acknowledge the assistance given by Smith & Wesson; the Library of Congress; the National Archives; the Connecticut Valley Historical Museum; Stuart W. Pyhrr of the Department of Arms and Armor, The Metropolitan Museum of Art; David A Cardé and Chris Gallo of Greg Martin Auctions; Walt Goulet; and especially Jim Supica. Picture credits have been acknowledged with the captions. Where no credit has been given this indicates the photograph has been drawn from the archives of Salamander Books. The publishers are grateful for the assistance given by the Buffalo Bill Historical Center and the Gene Autry Western Heritage Museum, where some of the firearms were photographed.

Above: A fine Smith & Wesson Model .320 revolving rifle with detachable shoulder stock. (Courtesy Greg Martin Auctions.)

Page 1: Two of the 1,000 S&W Americans bought by the U.S. Army around 1871. (Courtesy Jim Supica.)

Page 3: Smith & Wesson .38 Safety Double Action revolver in steel, silver and enamel, made between 1890 and 1893. The revolver was shown by Smith & Wesson at the World's Columbian Exposition in Chicago in 1893. (The Gerald Klaz Trust Collection on exhibit at The Metropolitan Museum of Art, New York.)

Contents

Above: A Model 422 semi-automatic in .22 L.R., with non-factory scope and mount. (Courtesy Jim Supica.)

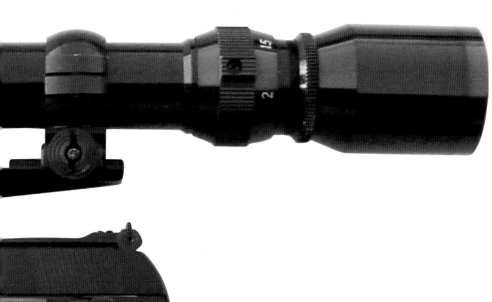

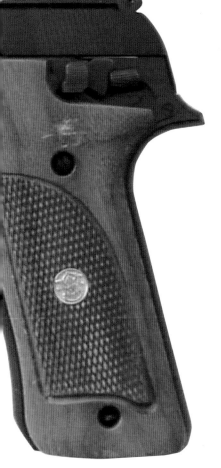

PREFACE

by Jim Supica, J.D.

The history of Smith & Wesson is nothing less than the history of the modern handgun. Over the past century and a half, S&W has been the world's predominant revolver maker, with a history of continuous innovation and quality manufacture.

The firm's beginnings in the mid-1800s coincided with, and in many ways provided the driving force for, the watershed event in firearms evolution — the development of a practical repeating gun firing self-contained metallic cartridges.

A few years before D. B. Wesson and Horace Smith forged their partnership, Samuel Colt had revolutionized small arms design with the introduction of a practical and dependable repeating firearm, the percussion revolver. While representing a tremendous advance over single-shot or double-barreled firearms, the use of the separate components of cap, ball, and black powder to load the weapon left significant room for improvement. The inventive genius of D. B. Wesson rose to the occasion, first with the development of a lever action design which eventually evolved into the Winchester repeating rifle, and then with the design of the first commercially successful American revolver to fire self-contained metallic cartridges – the tip-up S&W Model One.

From that auspicious beginning, the S&W milestones came with surprising regularity. Their top-break revolver design introduced in 1870 became arguably the predominant handgun pattern for the last quarter of that century, with millions of examples produced both by S&W and numerous other firms.

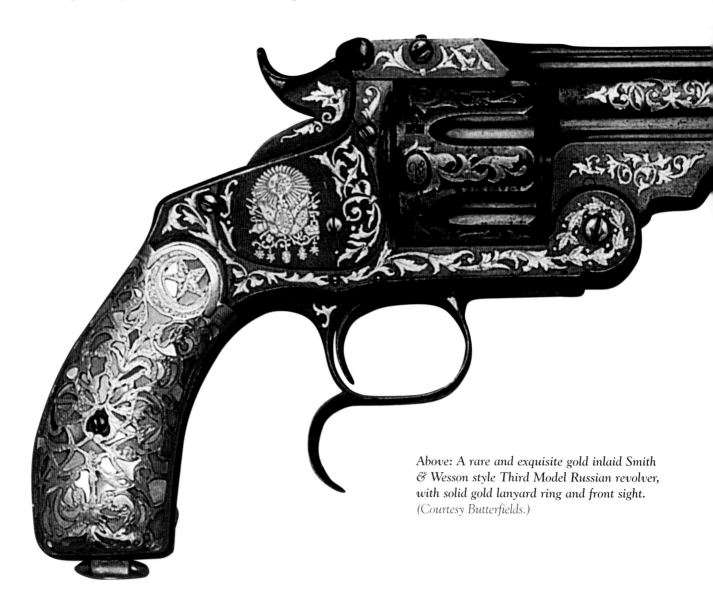

Above: A rare and exquisite gold inlaid Smith & Wesson style Third Model Russian revolver, with solid gold lanyard ring and front sight. (Courtesy Butterfields.)

While the classic Colt Single Action Army has captured the collective imagination as the quintessential sidearm of the late 1800s, it is interesting to note that production of the large solid frame Colt SAA models did not catch up with S&Ws large frame top-break Model Threes until well into the 20th century. In the American West, big Smiths at one time or another filled the holsters of such famous and infamous individuals as Frank and Jesse James, Cole Younger, Bill Tilghman, Dallas Stoudenmire, Texas Jack Omohundro, Virgil Earp, John Wesley Hardin, Pat Garrett, Buffalo Bill Cody, Annie Oakley, Gen. Leonard Wood, and Theodore Roosevelt.

In the 1890s, S&W followed rival Colt's lead in producing double action revolvers with swing-out cylinders. In the last year of that decade, the classic S&W Military and Police K-frame revolver was introduced, along with the .38 Special round. This gun and cartridge combination was destined to become the predominant sidearm for U.S. police forces of the 20th century, while its direct descendant, the Model 10, remained in production a hundred years later.

As with the .38 Special, many other S&W innovations were tied to the development of new cartridges, along with the guns to fire them. Some rounds such as the .32 S&W and .44 Special were noted for exceptional accuracy. Other S&W innovations in accuracy included the introduction and continual improvement of adjustable target sights, making the firm's products favorites with champion target shooters around the world. Previously unimagined power levels for a handgun were reached with the introduction of the .357 Magnum, and later topped with the .44 Magnum, with both innovations leading to the development of handgun hunting as a legitimate sporting pursuit.

Some S&W revolvers have gained near-cult followings, such as the massive Triplelock, the diminutive .22 LadySmith, the tack-driving K frame Target Masterpiece series, and the powerful Model 29 of "Dirty Harry" fame. Others have become so ubiquitous that their Model designations have come to nearly define a particular class of firearm, such as the Chiefs Special and the Kit Gun.

Smith and Wesson innovation has not been limited to revolvers. The company made the first American double action 9mm pistol, and introduced the world's first "wonder-nine," combining double action firing mechanism with high-capacity double stack magazine in a 9mm pistol. The .22 Model 41 is a target classic, and the introduction of the .40 S&W round has gained immense popularity for police and personal defense applications.

In the first years of the 21st century, the S&W tradition continues, with the world's most extensive handgun product line and innovative concepts such as their ultra-lightweight Scandium and Titanium frame revolvers. Under new ownership, Smith and Wesson, again American-made and American-owned, begins its second 150 years with a rich history and a bright future.

The history of this firearms giant has been recorded and preserved in some well-researched documents. However, given the dominance of S&W in the handgun world, I've always been surprised and a little disappointed that so few books have been published on the subject. As you may imagine, therefore, I learned of Dean Boorman's new book on the topic with excitement and anticipation. Dean's beautiful books on the history of Colt and Winchester firearms are outstanding works that have provided me much enjoyment. As president of the oldest gun collecting club in America, the Armour and Arms Club of New York, and as grand-nephew of the founder of the Department of Arms and Armor of the Metropolitan Museum of Art, Dean brings an appreciation of firearms history and gun collecting to this endeavor that enlivens the pages of this work. It takes a place with the works of such well-respected S&W writers as Roy Jinks, Robert Neal, John Parsons, Charles Pate, Richard Nahas, Martin Rywell, and David Chicoine as an important and enjoyable work in this fascinating field.

INTRODUCTION

Referring to his .44 Magnum in the movie "Dirty Harry," Clint Eastwood says, "This is the most powerful handgun in the world." Meanwhile, an automobile bumper sticker shouts, "Insured by Smith & Wesson." These phrases evoke the fame of the Smith & Wesson trademark. Indeed, this is the first name that comes to mind in regard to the modern pistol, whether for the police, for self-defense, or for competitive target shooting.

The company may certainly be recognized as the premier handgun manufacturer in the United States, and indeed the world. Company marketing director Ken Jorgensen estimates that it makes some 20 percent of all handguns sold worldwide. The company's 2002 sales brochure showed no fewer than 65 models of revolvers and 76 semi-automatics.

As this book was being written, the company was celebrating its 150th anniversary. Horace Smith and Daniel B. Wesson formed their first partnership in 1852, and since then, through the Industrial Revolution, wars, and times of prosperity and depression, not to mention the current "gun control" movement, it is "solid and secure with products known for innovation, quality, value and reliability," in Jorgensen's words. Together with Colt and Winchester, also products of Connecticut Valley Yankee drive and ingenuity, the company represents America's historic leadership in the firearms field.

The company's beginnings are remarkably similar to those of Colt and Winchester, except that the partnership of Smith and Wesson was one of two compatible equals. All three companies experienced initial failures, then monopoly through innovative patents, expansion into worldwide markets, and boom and bust cycles in World Wars I and II. At the same time all three companies produced firearms of outstanding quality and effectiveness as well as esthetic appeal, creating a fertile field for both antique and modern

Above: One of the most famous of all Smith & Wesson handguns is the Model 29 .44in Magnum, for its association with the "Dirty Harry" movies.

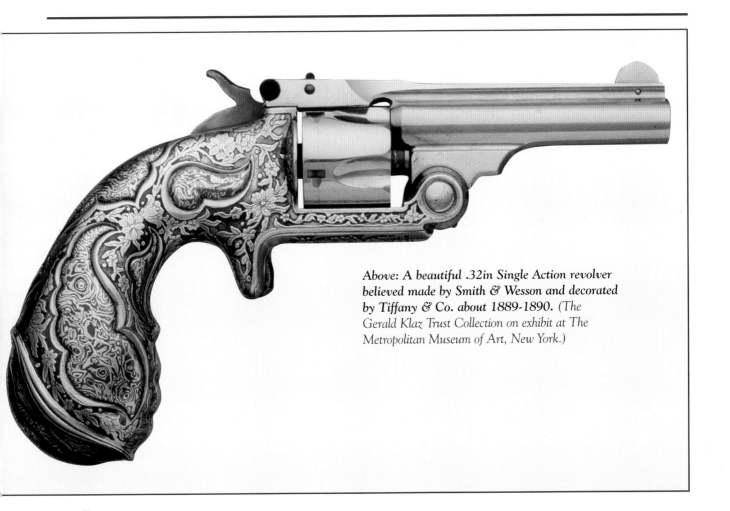

Above: A beautiful .32in Single Action revolver believed made by Smith & Wesson and decorated by Tiffany & Co. about 1889-1890. (The Gerald Klaz Trust Collection on exhibit at The Metropolitan Museum of Art, New York.)

arms collectors (and investors, in terms of increase in value).

This book is intended to provide an overview of Smith & Wesson firearms from the beginning to the present time, not so much as a technical reference as has been done by others, but in the context of how the guns were developed, how they were used, and the historical background of the people who were involved in the company and in the use of these arms. There is a daunting variety of models and types of Smith & Wesson handguns which has persisted to this day. An effort is made here to sort these out into a coherent pattern. At the same time, a record is presented with color photographs of the major types of Smith & Wesson handguns, and examples with particular historic associations or with high decoration, together with the background of the historic periods involved.

The chapters which follow are arranged generally in chronological order instead of by gun models, although there is necessarily some overlap as various models were sold over a long period of years. For example, over six million revolvers based on the Military & Police Model of 1899 have been sold to date, and are still shown in the company's sales brochures.

The first chapter deals with the formation of the original partnership and how its lever-action repeating pistol later developed into the Winchester lever-action rifle. The next relates the partnership's breakthrough with the first practical revolver with a self-contained cartridge, establishing a

Above: The .38 Military & Police First Model adopted by the U.S. Army as their Model 1899, eventually evolving into the quintessential police firearm of the mid-20th century. (Courtesy ArmchairGunShow.com)

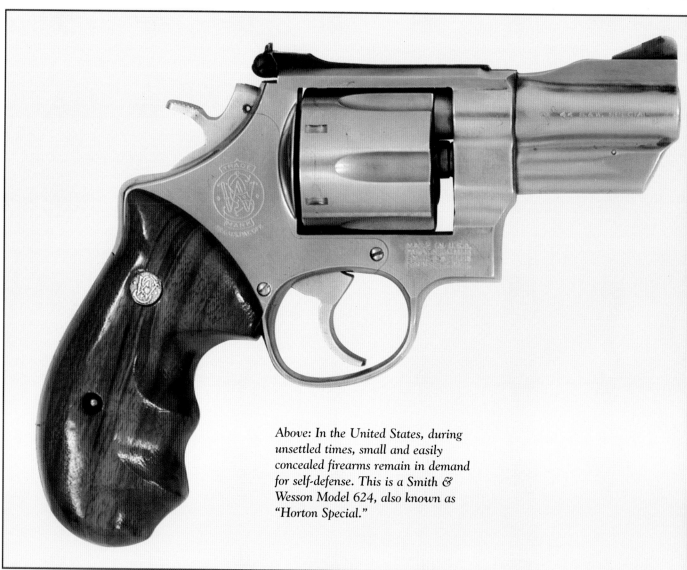

Above: In the United States, during unsettled times, small and easily concealed firearms remain in demand for self-defense. This is a Smith & Wesson Model 624, also known as "Horton Special."

and particularly the development of the innovative .357 Magnum cartridge and revolver, together with the first attempts at a semi-automatic pistol. It covers the special models and extensive domestic and overseas sales made during World War II and also the specialty models developed for the military as recently as for the Vietnam War and the Cold War, a period of much innovation, particularly as regards the "Dirty Harry" .44 Magnum and the 9mm semi-automatic of the type which has now become a police and military standard. This period also saw the evolution of the company's ownership through successive control by industrial conglomerates to its present new ownership as a single-purpose American corporation. The company's recent innovations and current offerings, as well as the other facilities it provides, such as the Performance Center (custom gun shop), the Shooting Sports Center, and the Smith and Wesson Academy, are described in the next chapter.

The immensely enjoyable field of collecting antique Smith & Wessons in terms of how values have increased, the dealers and gun shows, and the major arms museums where examples may be seen are covered in the next chapter. Reference is made to the "gun control" as it relates to collectors, and information is provided on the Smith & Wesson Collectors Association. The final chapter then describes a firing test of a collection of representative Smith & Wessons with a subjective evaluation of their accuracy and power.

The company is to be commended for its support for research into its history. Much of this research has been drawn on in the preparation of this book. This is especially so of the books by the company historian Roy Jinks, including *Smith & Wesson 1857-1945* (with Robert Neal), and *The History of Smith & Wesson* (1977). A further major resource has been *The Standard Catalog of Smith & Wesson*, by Jim Supica and Richard Nahas. In addition, the company sponsors an annual magazine, *Smith & Wesson Handguns*, its 2002 edition celebrating the company's 150th anniversary, with a series of valuable articles by leading gun writers.

Many individuals have contributed greatly to this book. These include Ken Jorgensen, marketing and communications director at Smith & Wesson; Jim Supica, author as referred to above, and proprietor of Old Town Station Antique Firearms, Lenexa, KS, who contributed a splendid collection of photographs as well as the preface to this book; John Hamilton, retired director, and Guy McLain, present director, of the Connecticut Valley Historical Museum; Walt Goulet of the Ohio Gun Collectors Association; and Jay Hansen of Hansen and Hansen, Southport, CT, antique firearms. Thanks are also due to Angus Laidlaw, a contributing editor of *American Rifleman* magazine, who shared his excellent library and led our informal shooting demonstration team.

monopoly that extended through the Civil War. The third chapter covers the period from then until the turn of the century, with the development of the top-break large caliber revolver, which met with huge success overseas and was a competitor of Colt's in the Old West.

The next chapter takes up the period from the late 1800s through World War I, when the company made its major advances with swing-out cylinder ("Hand Ejector") revolvers and the .38 Special cartridge. The fifth chapter explains the shifting fortunes of the company in the interwar period of the Roaring Twenties and the Great Depression,

EARLY PARTNERSHIPS

It can all be said to have started when George Washington ordered the construction of two National Armories in 1795. The Revolutionary War had ended not long before, and the Continental Army had had to make do with obsolete French muskets, since the British had not allowed the development of manufacturing in America. As locations not exposed to raids by British warships and having water power available, Washington chose Springfield, Massachusetts, and Harper's Ferry, Virginia (he had an interest in the Chesapeake and Ohio Canal which served the latter). Both armories became prime sources of industrial innovation, Harper's Ferry sponsoring the first breechloading rifle, the Hall, and Springfield pioneering large-scale production with new machinery. Unlike in England, which had a network of cottage industries producing parts, the Americans did not have an established labor force, and had a stronger incentive to have machines replace individual workers.

Horace Smith was born in 1808. His father, Silas, was employed as a carpenter at the Springfield Armory. Young Horace went to work there at the age of sixteen as an apprentice helper to a bayonet forger. He remained at the Armory for eighteen years, becoming a journeyman working in various departments. He is given credit for inventing several types of gunmaking machinery, such as a special machine for checkering hammers. From about 1842 to 1851, Smith worked for various gunmaking firms in Connecticut and Massachusetts, and also produced firearms in his own shop. One of these was a bizarre repeating pistol with three separate magazines, for ball, for powder, and for primers. It was not practical, but an effort to compete with the only two systems of repeating guns available at the time, the pepperbox (an inaccurate, low-powered arrangement of revolving barrels), and the new Colt revolver first patented in 1836.

Daniel Baird Wesson was born in 1825, and was thus seventeen years younger than Horace Smith, a difference in age which apparently produced almost a father and son relationship between the two. Wesson's father was a farmer, but Daniel's older brother Edwin was established as a gunsmith and riflemaker with a shop in Grafton, Massachusetts. Daniel showed an early interest in the mechanics of firearms such that in 1842, at the age of seventeen, he was glad to enter into an indenture arrangement so that he could go to work for his brother instead of on his father's farm. Edwin agreed to pay the father $250 in order for Daniel to work for him for 3½ years.

Left: Horace Smith was born in 1808. He designed and made machinery for making guns, as well as the guns themselves, and eventually became a very successful businessman. (Courtesy Connecticut Valley Historical Museum.)

Daniel's period of apprenticeship was an excellent education. He took part in the manufacture of his brother's target rifles, considered the finest in the world, and personally negotiated with Samuel Colt on Colt's purchase of barrels from Edwin's company for the new Walker Dragoon pistols. He also became familiar with patents and the problem of infringement, when Edwin's invention of the false muzzle for target rifles, which made them more accurate by better seating of the bullet, was stolen by competitors. However, disaster struck: shortly after Daniel's apprenticeship expired in 1849, Edwin died of a sudden heart attack. With large unpaid debts, the company went bankrupt, and Daniel had to sue to recover even his gunsmith's tools.

Right: As well as forging a famous and fruitful business partnership with Horace Smith, Daniel Wesson headed up a dynasty that would be intimately involved in the company's management for almost a hundred years.

Below: Edwin Wesson, Daniel's older brother, made this Percussion Boy's Rifle during the period 1837-1839 while at a shop in Grafton, Massachusetts. Of .393in caliber, it has a 27³/₄in octagonal barrel with eight-groove rifling.

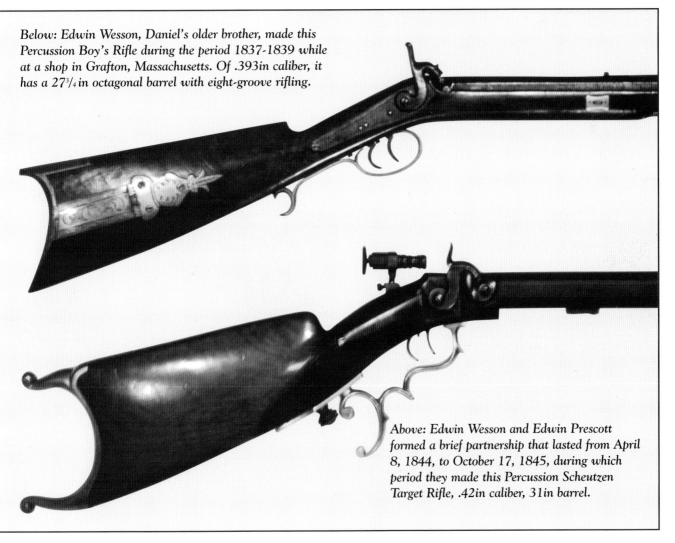

Above: Edwin Wesson and Edwin Prescott formed a brief partnership that lasted from April 8, 1844, to October 17, 1845, during which period they made this Percussion Scheutzen Target Rifle, .42in caliber, 31in barrel.

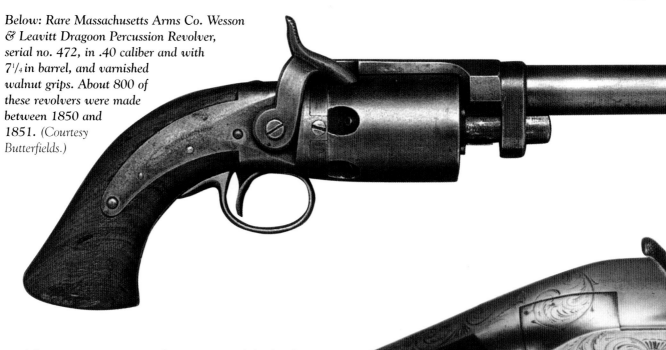

Below: Rare Massachusetts Arms Co. Wesson & Leavitt Dragoon Percussion Revolver, serial no. 472, in .40 caliber and with 7¼ in barrel, and varnished walnut grips. About 800 of these revolvers were made between 1850 and 1851. (Courtesy Butterfields.)

After trying again to manufacture guns with his brothers Franklin and Martin, he worked for other companies including the Massachusetts Arms Company, which tried producing the Leavitt revolver but lost a patent infringement suit by Colt. Then, in 1850, Horace Smith and Daniel Wesson came together to work on a newly patented repeating rifle being produced at the Robbins and Lawrence factory in Windsor, Vermont.

The Springfield and Harper's Ferry Armory heritage of what came to be known as the "American System" of mass production by machine tools came full circle at Robbins and Lawrence. Neither of the two armories nor the progressive gun manufacturers Hall and Eli Whitney had succeeded in producing firearms with fully interchangeable parts. Robbins and Lawrence (originally Robbins, Kendall and Lawrence) were the first to do so, with its successful contract in 1844 for 10,000 Harper's Ferry type U.S. Army rifles. The machinery designed at the factory for this was so successful that a British delegation bought a set for its Enfield Armory. Instead of a skilled gunsmith making an entire gun, less skilled workmen could now use machines to work just on separate parts. A comparable advance in its time to present-day computerized technology, this opened new opportunities for entrepreneurs like Smith and Wesson.

The Hunt and Jennings rifle

Walter Hunt, a brilliant New York inventor (responsible for the safety pin and the lock-stitch needle on the sewing machine) took out a patent in 1849 for a rifle he called the Volitional Repeater. This incorporated the basic features of the modern lever-action rifle: a tubular magazine under the barrel, a lever mechanism to raise the cartridges into the chamber, and a kind of cartridge, a combination of a bullet

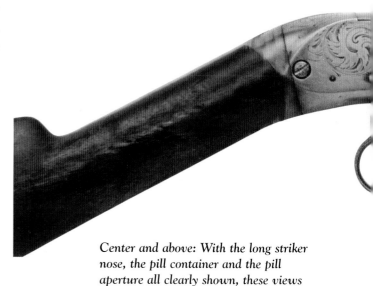

Center and above: With the long striker nose, the pill container and the pill aperture all clearly shown, these views show the Jennings rifle cocked and ready to fire (top), and with the hammer down.

and gunpowder set off by a firing pin. Unable to finance his production, Hunt sold his rights to George Arrowsmith, who had his employee, Lewis Jennings, simplify and improve the mechanism. Courtland Palmer, a wealthy New York hardware merchant, joined Arrowsmith to place an order for Jennings patent rifles at Robbins and Lawrence.

The new rifle did not sell well and production was curtailed, largely due to the lack of an effective cartridge.

Hunt's original invention included the use of what he called "Rocket Ball," a bullet with a hollow base containing the gunpowder. This arrangement lacked power and tended to erode the rifle barrel. Also, the gun was subject to the bullet being stuck in the barrel, with no effective means of ejection. Most of the rifles produced were actually converted to single shot. Horace Smith and Daniel Wesson, who were working at Robbins and Lawrence, developed three more models, this time all as repeaters referred to as the Smith-Jennings Rifle, but still with limited success.

The lever-action pistol

In what must have been an extensive series of discussions between Horace Smith and Daniel Wesson, it was agreed that the low-powered "Rocket Ball" would be more appropriate for a pistol than for a rifle, and also that there might be a better way to combine the bullet, the gunpowder, and the primer. A French inventor, Flobert, had already patented a simple system which he used for his "saloon pistol" for indoor target practice. This was simply a copper percussion cap with a small lead ball seated inside. Percussion caps were in common use for single-shot rifles, muskets, and pistols, having replaced the earlier flintlock system of ignition. With a flintlock, the main charge of powder and the bullet are loaded into the gun from the muzzle. There is an exterior pan for priming powder, connected to the main charge by a touch hole. The priming powder is ignited by a piece of flint held in the jaws of the hammer, striking a hinged "frizzen" over the pan. With the percussion cap system, a tube is inserted through the touch hole with a nipple on the outside end on which a percussion cap is placed, this being set off by being struck by the hammer when the gun's trigger is pulled.

The "Rocket Ball" was only a part measure toward a self contained cartridge. It still required an exterior primer to ignite the powder inside the bullet, which is why the Hunt and Jennings rifles had exterior hammers to set off separate percussion caps or disc primers. What was needed, and what

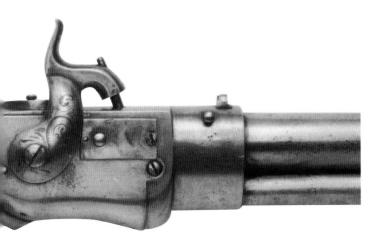

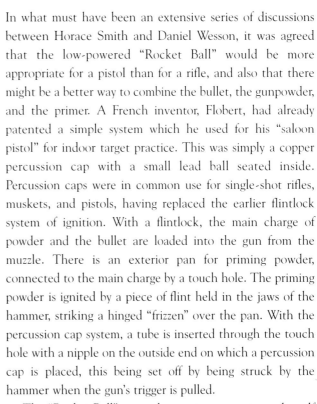

LEVER-ACTION REPEATING PISTOL

Type: tubular magazine under barrel; steel frame, blued.

Caliber and capacity: .31 (Model 1), 7 rounds; .41 (Model 2), 10 rounds.

Barrel length: Model 1, 4in; Model 2, 8in.

Manufactured: 1854-55.

Quantity: Model 1, approx. 1,208; Model 2, under 500.

Markings: Smith & Wesson, Cast Steel Patented, Norwich, CT.

Variations: individual variations in parts and style of markings. There are later Model 2s with 6in barrels and a pistol carbine with a 16in barrel.

Ammunition: Flobert type rimfire cartridge or "Rocket Ball" type with gunpowder inside.

Mechanical function: magazine loaded from front; forward movement of trigger guard lever moves cartridge up into the chamber.

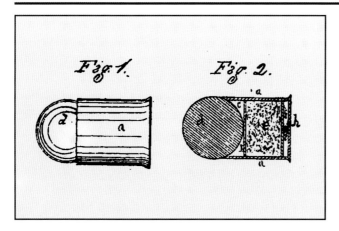

Above: Some of the drawings related to the August 8, 1854, patent by Horace Smith and Daniel Wesson for an "improved cartridge for pistols, rifles or other firearms. Fig. 2 "represents the cylindrical case of the cartridge, which may be made of thin plate-copper or any other suitable material."

was patented by Horace Smith and Daniel Wesson in 1853 and 1854, was a larger version of the Flobert cartridge with powder as well as a primer, and an extension of the lever-action mechanism in which moving the lever, as well as ejecting a used cartridge and seating a new cartridge, would cock a bolt with a spring-loaded firing pin actuated by the trigger.

This was such a revolutionary invention that the two decided to set up their own company, and Courtland Palmer agreed to provide the financing. Their first factory was

established in Norwich, Connecticut. Here were produced the two pistols of the first Smith & Wesson partnership. While the pistols were beautifully made and ingenious in their design, they were not entirely successful: the new cartridge did not work well, and was replaced by an updated version of the "Rocket Ball," incorporating a primer in the base. The multi-shot capacity, however, was startling: the only other effective repeating firearm available at the time was the Colt percussion revolver, which was good for six shots without reloading, but then required a cumbersome loading process involving a separate bullet, charge of powder, and percussion cap. The new lever-action gun acquired the nickname of the Volcanic since it was compared to the eruption of a volcano; this may have derived from an article in the magazine *Scientific American* in 1854.

The story of the new gun after 1855 becomes the story of the Winchester rifle. Struggling financially, the partnership formed by Smith and Wesson received a buyout offer from a

Below and opposite page: Some of the drawings supporting the February 14, 1854, patent (No. 10,535) of H. Smith and D. B. Wesson who, according to the specification, "have invented certain new and useful Improvements in Guns, Pistols, or Fire-Arms." Fig. 4 shows a side view of the kind of cartridge they intended to be used, "it being the same as is used in that species of pistols usually termed the 'Saloon pistol,' it being, as we believe, a French invention." This was Flobert's self-contained cartridge using a lead ball seated in a copper percussion cap. It became the .22in rimfire cartridge.

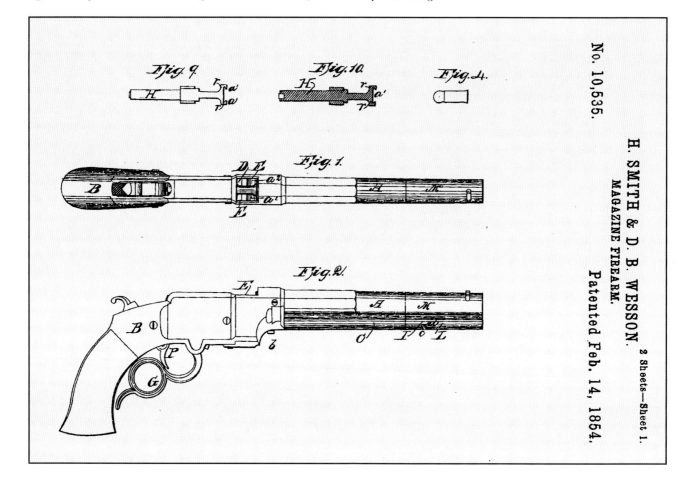

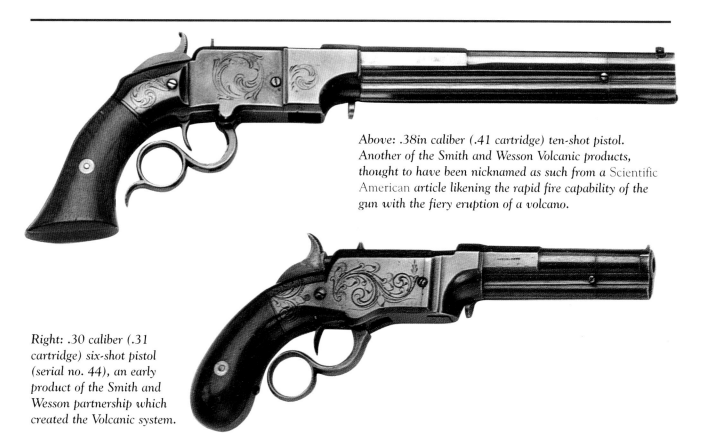

Above: .38in caliber (.41 cartridge) ten-shot pistol. Another of the Smith and Wesson Volcanic products, thought to have been nicknamed as such from a Scientific American article likening the rapid fire capability of the gun with the fiery eruption of a volcano.

Right: .30 caliber (.31 cartridge) six-shot pistol (serial no. 44), an early product of the Smith and Wesson partnership which created the Volcanic system.

group of investors including Oliver Winchester, a successful New Haven, CT, merchant and shirtmaker. Daniel Wesson stayed on for a while as general manager while the factory moved to New Haven. Pistols, and also rifles, were made under the name of the Volcanic Repeating Arms Company. However, this company ran into financial difficulties and went bankrupt, with Oliver Winchester acquiring all of its rights and property. He engaged a brilliant new plant superintendent, Benjamin Tyler Henry (previously foreman at Robbins & Lawrence), who developed the .44 rimfire cartridge and the Henry rifle, laying the foundation for the Winchester, one of the "Guns That Won the West."

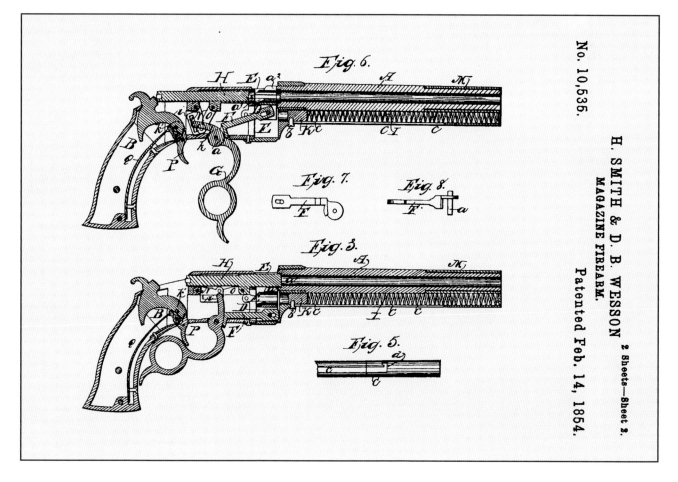

THE CARTRIDGE REVOLVER THROUGH THE CIVIL WAR

With the end of the first Smith and Wesson partnership in 1855, Horace Smith moved back to his home town of Springfield, Massachusetts, to work for his brother-in-law's livery stable. Daniel Wesson, however, still involved as plant manager for the company now producing Volcanic pistols, continued to develop his self-contained cartridge, and turned to the idea of using this for a revolver instead of a lever-action pistol. His first attempt was to make a wooden model of a .22 caliber version.

Colt's patent for the revolver, which had given that company a monopoly on its percussion cap operated pistols and rifles since 1836, was expiring in 1856, so there was no problem in using the revolver mechanism. Colt had solved the problem of having the hammer at the rear of the gun revolve the cylinder when cocked, with the cylinder locked in place for the next shot. What Colt failed to do, however, was to anticipate the use of self-contained cartridges fired by the hammer, requiring the chambers in the cylinder to be bored all the way through. Under the percussion system, the powder and ball were loaded from the front and held by a solid partition behind, pierced only by a touch hole leading to the percussion cap.

Rollin White, an employee of Colt's, had tried unsuccessfully to interest his company in the concept of the bored through cylinder, so in 1855 took out a patent on the idea himself, as part of an impractical proposal for a magazine-loaded repeating pistol. Daniel Wesson saw that the use of this patent was needed for his revolver, and late in 1856, bringing Horace Smith back into the picture, secured an agreement with Rollin White (who had by then left Colt's) to use the patent on payment of a royalty of 25 cents per gun. White was committed under this agreement to defend against patent infringements, which turned out to be expensive for him but advantageous to Smith and Wesson. Roy Jinks points out that Wesson may have used Smith's name for this agreement without even consulting him, banking on their friendship. In any event, the new Smith & Wesson Company was formed, opened its factory in Springfield, and went into full production of its Model 1 .22in caliber pistols in 1858. It moved to a larger factory on

Below: One of the drawings associated with the patent (No. 14147) granted to Horace Smith and D. B. Wesson on January 22, 1856, for a Volcanic-style .22in caliber revolver cartridge.

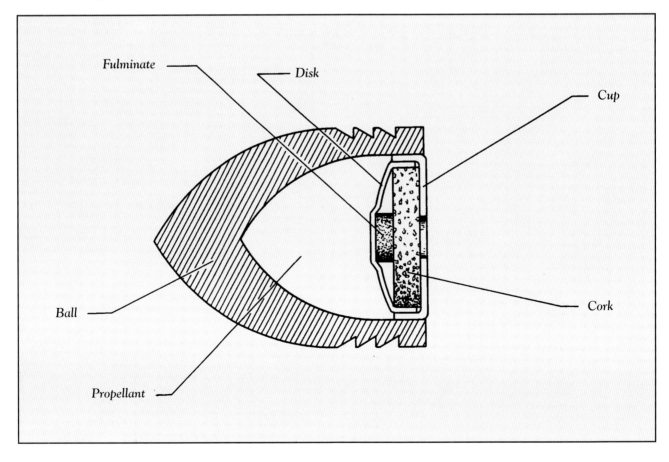

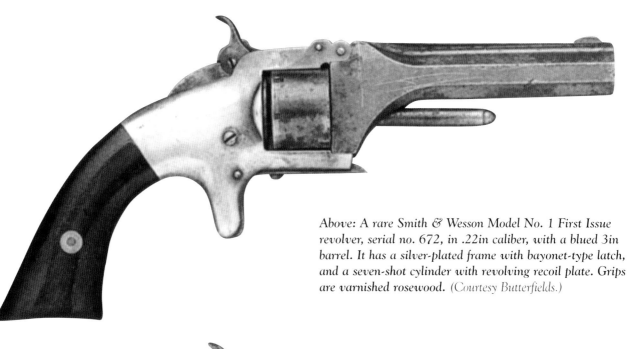

Above: A rare Smith & Wesson Model No. 1 First Issue revolver, serial no. 672, in .22in caliber, with a blued 3in barrel. It has a silver-plated frame with bayonet-type latch, and a seven-shot cylinder with revolving recoil plate. Grips are varnished rosewood. (Courtesy Butterfields.)

Above: A Model No. 1 Second Issue revolver, serial no. 84898, in .22in caliber, with a 3¹/₈in barrel marked "Smith & Wesson Springfield Mass." The cylinder has three patent dates. The revolver is blued overall, with varnished rosewood grips. (Courtesy Butterfields.)

Right: An imposing factory building for a successful business: Smith & Wesson's plant in Stockbridge Street, Springfield, Massachusetts. (Courtesy Connecticut Valley Historical Museum.)

Stockbridge Street, near the Springfield Armory, in 1859. "The rest is history." The same company remains in Springfield, Massachusetts, to this day, relocated to a newer factory on Roosevelt Boulevard.

There was an immediate market for this innovative handgun, not only in the urban areas of the Northeast, but also in the West, where discovery of gold in 1849 had produced a new rush of population, and also in the Middle West, where the simmering struggle with the South over the issue of slavery had stimulated bloody clashes in Kansas. The diminutive Model 1 used what is still known as the .22 Short cartridge; it is a testimony to Smith & Wesson's inventiveness that the same cartridge, with smokeless instead of black powder, is still made today. While it had limited power, it was still lethal at short range as a "hideout" weapon.

The Model 1 First Issue was difficult to manufacture, with a brass frame and a small sideplate accessing its inner workings. In 1860 the gun was substantially redesigned with a steel frame and a large sideplate. It remained mechanically unchanged but had a facelift in appearance in 1868, and continued in production all the way up to 1882.

Left: The Model 1 evolved through three major variations. The First Issue (top) is identified by its hinged hammer spur, rounded side frame, and circular side plate. The Second Issue (middle) went to an integral hammer spur, flat-sided frame, and large irregular side plate. The Third Issue changed the octagon barrel to round, fluted the previously unfluted cylinder, and changed to a rounded "bird's head" butt configuration. (Courtesy ArmchairGunShow.com.)

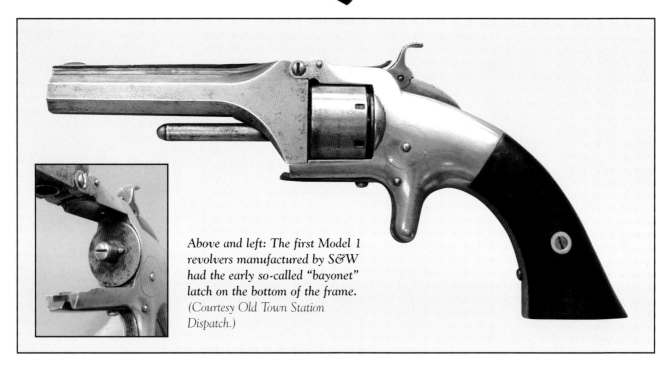

Above and left: The first Model 1 revolvers manufactured by S&W had the early so-called "bayonet" latch on the bottom of the frame. (Courtesy Old Town Station Dispatch.)

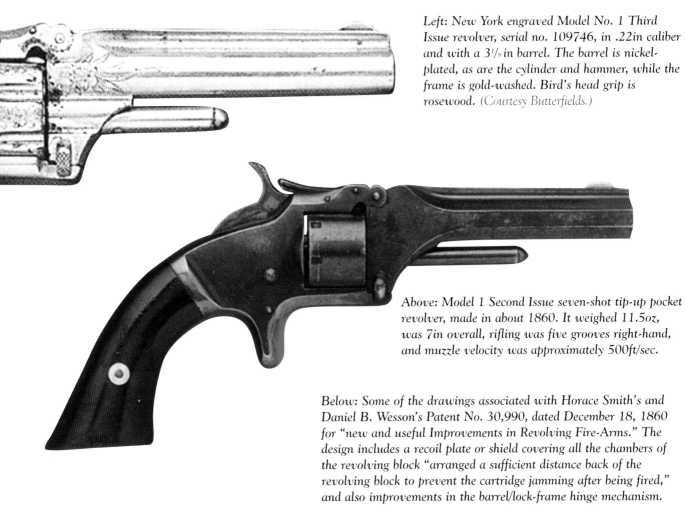

Left: New York engraved Model No. 1 Third Issue revolver, serial no. 109746, in .22in caliber and with a 3¹/₈in barrel. The barrel is nickel-plated, as are the cylinder and hammer, while the frame is gold-washed. Bird's head grip is rosewood. (Courtesy Butterfields.)

Above: Model 1 Second Issue seven-shot tip-up pocket revolver, made in about 1860. It weighed 11.5oz, was 7in overall, rifling was five grooves right-hand, and muzzle velocity was approximately 500ft/sec.

Below: Some of the drawings associated with Horace Smith's and Daniel B. Wesson's Patent No. 30,990, dated December 18, 1860 for "new and useful Improvements in Revolving Fire-Arms." The design includes a recoil plate or shield covering all the chambers of the revolving block "arranged a sufficient distance back of the revolving block to prevent the cartridge jamming after being fired," and also improvements in the barrel/lock-frame hinge mechanism.

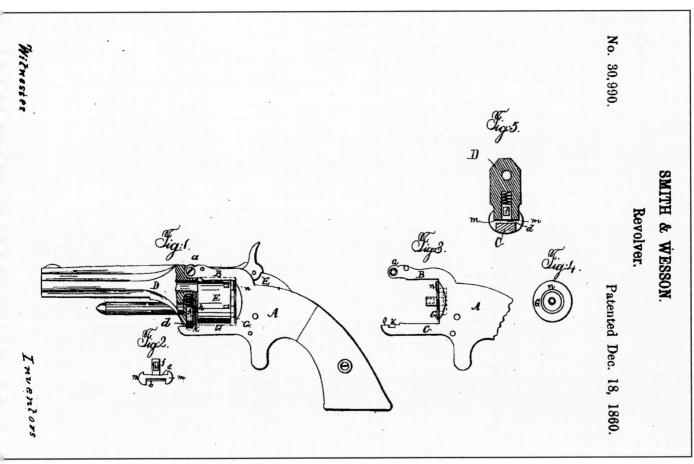

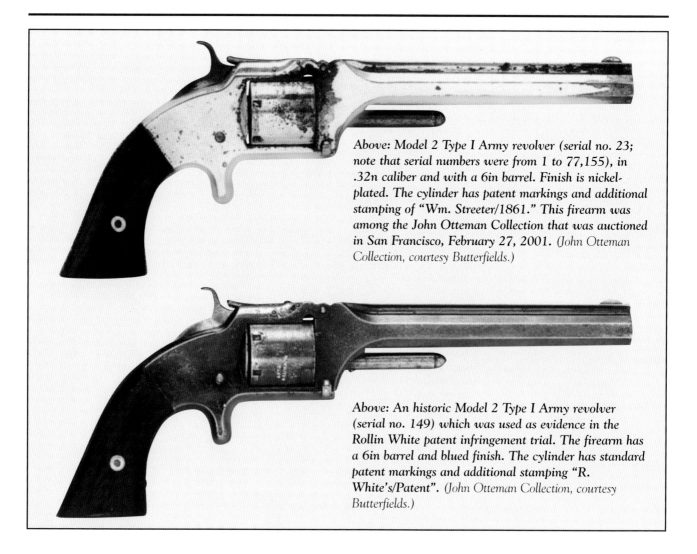

Above: Model 2 Type I Army revolver (serial no. 23; note that serial numbers were from 1 to 77,155), in .32n caliber and with a 6in barrel. Finish is nickel-plated. The cylinder has patent markings and additional stamping of "Wm. Streeter/1861." This firearm was among the John Otteman Collection that was auctioned in San Francisco, February 27, 2001. (John Otteman Collection, courtesy Butterfields.)

Above: An historic Model 2 Type I Army revolver (serial no. 149) which was used as evidence in the Rollin White patent infringement trial. The firearm has a 6in barrel and blued finish. The cylinder has standard patent markings and additional stamping "R. White's/Patent". (John Otteman Collection, courtesy Butterfields.)

The two partners began developing a larger caliber pistol as soon as the new company was formed, the main problem being the redesign of the cartridge. The Model 2, in .32in caliber was introduced in June, 1861, with most fortunate timing, just two months before the firing on Fort Sumter in Charleston Harbor, South Carolina, which began the Civil War.

The Model 2 Army, as the pistol came to be known, was so well designed that it remained in production with practically no modification up to 1874. At the beginning of the Civil War, as Roy Jinks relates, "Fear of invasion gripped the North, and northern soldiers were searching for compact arms to carry to war . . . the Model 2 was perfectly suited, meeting the demands of a belt-sized pistol that could be carried in the waistband or small holster. It could be quickly loaded with the new waterproof metallic cartridges and it proved ideal for the soldiers as well as those on the home front." The volume of demand was such that the company was forced to stop taking new orders in 1862 because its production capacity had been reached.

It might be questioned why the U.S. government did not step in and engage more manufacturers, as happened with rifles and pistols in World Wars I and II, instead of the soldiers having to buy these pistols themselves, from a limited supply. Unfortunately, at the time the Ordnance

Department had no research and development branch and was headed by the stubborn, conservative General James W. Ripley. His lack of interest in new developments extended over the entire arms field; he was finally relieved in 1863. However, the Ordnance Department did adopt the Colt Army percussion pistol in .44in caliber, which was more powerful than the Smith & Wesson Model 2. The Colt .31in Pocket Model and .36in caliber Navy Colts were popular for private purchase by the troops although, like the .44in model, were percussion muzzleloaders. While the war made handguns widely popular, the Union could have brought the conflict to an earlier end by taking advantage of advances, particularly in longarms.

The State of Kentucky, more progressive than the Union Army, did purchase 2,600 Model 2s in 1863 through Cincinnati dealer B. Kittredge & Co., and issued them to the Kentucky Cavalry. These were marked Kittredge on the barrel, and bring a premium in the collectors' market.

The Model 2 Army was widely used in the Old West. Most famously, "Wild Bill" Hickok was carrying one when as marshal of Deadwood he was shot to death while playing cards with the "dead man's hand," aces and eights. George Armstrong Custer was presented with a decorated pair, which is on display at the Gene Autry Western Heritage Museum in Los Angeles, California.

The Wesson name

The company prospered, and by 1865 Horace Smith and Daniel Webster were taking out salaries of $160,000 each, the most of anyone in the city of Springfield. Daniel Wesson must have chuckled: when he married Cynthia Hawes in 1849, her father objected because he felt Wesson was only a gunsmith and had no future, and the couple had to elope. Over the years, until his death, "D.B." built and endowed two major city hospitals and founded a scholarship fund for college students which remains active today. Horace Smith also contributed to major city charities.

At this point it may be useful to explain the relationship to Smith & Wesson of other companies with the Wesson name, whose products may be encountered by collectors. The earliest, as explained in the preceding chapter, was the Wesson Rifle Company, formed after the bankruptcy of the gunmaking shop operated by Daniel Wesson's older brother Edwin. This shop produced fine single-shot percussion rifles and pistols marked E. Wesson, from the early 1840s up to Edwin's death in 1849; production was under 150 rifles per year. Edwin also made a few Wesson, Stevens and Miller dragoon revolvers in 1848 under Daniel Leavitt's patent.

Horace Smith and Daniel Wesson made a short-lived venture into producing a fine shotgun that D.B. had invented. About 225 were produced between 1867 and

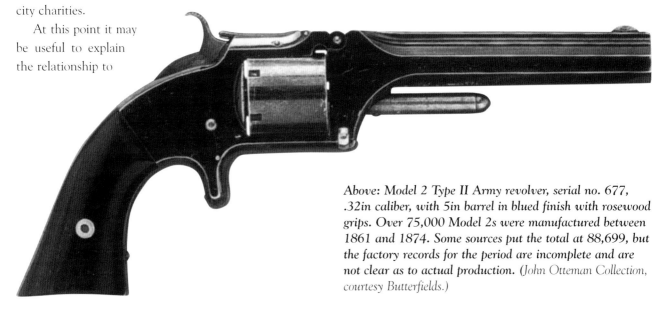

Above: Model 2 Type II Army revolver, serial no. 677, .32in caliber, with 5in barrel in blued finish with rosewood grips. Over 75,000 Model 2s were manufactured between 1861 and 1874. Some sources put the total at 88,699, but the factory records for the period are incomplete and are not clear as to actual production. (John Otteman Collection, courtesy Butterfields.)

Left: N. C. Wyeth's painting of "Wild Bill" Hickok unmasking a card cheat. When Hickok was murdered while playing poker in Deadwood in 1876, he was reported to have been carrying a Smith & Wesson Model 2 Army revolver.

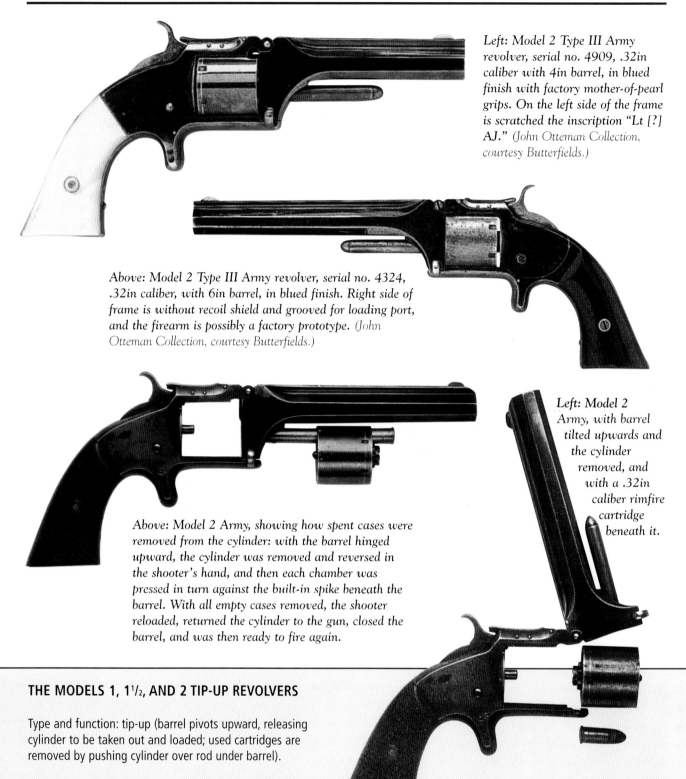

Left: Model 2 Type III Army revolver, serial no. 4909, .32in caliber with 4in barrel, in blued finish with factory mother-of-pearl grips. On the left side of the frame is scratched the inscription "Lt [?] AJ." (John Otteman Collection, courtesy Butterfields.)

Above: Model 2 Type III Army revolver, serial no. 4324, .32in caliber, with 6in barrel, in blued finish. Right side of frame is without recoil shield and grooved for loading port, and the firearm is possibly a factory prototype. (John Otteman Collection, courtesy Butterfields.)

Left: Model 2 Army, with barrel tilted upwards and the cylinder removed, and with a .32in caliber rimfire cartridge beneath it.

Above: Model 2 Army, showing how spent cases were removed from the cylinder: with the barrel hinged upward, the cylinder was removed and reversed in the shooter's hand, and then each chamber was pressed in turn against the built-in spike beneath the barrel. With all empty cases removed, the shooter reloaded, returned the cylinder to the gun, closed the barrel, and was then ready to fire again.

THE MODELS 1, 1¹/₂, AND 2 TIP-UP REVOLVERS

Type and function: tip-up (barrel pivots upward, releasing cylinder to be taken out and loaded; used cartridges are removed by pushing cylinder over rod under barrel).

Caliber and capacity: Model 1, .22in, seven shots; Model 2, .32in, six shots; Model 1¹/₂, .32in, five shots.

Barrel lengths: Model 1, 3³/₁₆in, Third Issue also 2¹¹/₁₆in; Model 1¹/₂ and 2, 3¹/₂in to 10in.

Manufactured: Model 1 First Issue, 1857-1860, Second Issue 1860-1868, Third Issue 1868-1882; Model 2, 1861-1874; Model 1¹/₂, 1865-1875.

Quantity: Model 1 First Issue, approx. 11,000; Second Issue, approx. 115,400; Third issue, 131,163; Model 2, 77,155; Model 1¹/₂, approx. 127,000.

Markings: Smith & Wesson, Springfield, MA, and patent dates; serial numbers on butt.

Variations: Model 1 First and Second Issue, 1857-1868, square butt and plain cylinder; Third Issue, bird's head butt and fluted cylinder. Model 2, first 3,000 had two pins for the top strap, after that three. Model 1¹/₂ First Issue square butt; Second Issue, bird's head butt with plain cylinder and barrel; Third Issue, fluted cylinder and barrel.

1871, under the name of the Wesson Firearms Company.

Daniel Wesson's brother Frank, three years younger, also did his apprenticeship under their older brother Edwin, but apparently emigrated to California to follow the Gold Rush after Edwin's death. In the late 1850s he returned to Worcester, Massachusetts, where he went into the gunmaking business under his own name. From 1859 to 1888, he produced two-trigger rifles and carbines, some of which were used by the military in the Civil War; the front trigger released the barrel to tip up for loading. He also produced under-lever falling block Wessons and single-shot and Deringer type pistols. He also joined with his cousin Gilbert Harrington starting in 1871, and this partnership was the predecessor to the Harrington and Richardson Arms Company, which was a major producer of single-shot pistols, revolvers, and sporting arms until 1986.

The Wesson name appears today, but with no connection to Smith & Wesson, in the Dan Wesson Firearms Company. This company was formed by a Wesson grandson, who had worked at Smith & Wesson in the 1960s, but has gone through different ownerships, with the founder no longer in the picture. Its line of pistols was noted in a recent issue of *American Rifleman* magazine.

Coming back to Smith & Wesson, its Model 1½ was introduced during the Civil War as a scaled-down version of the Model 2, to provide a pocket pistol of a larger caliber than the .22in Model 1. It was also more streamlined, so as to be withdrawn quickly from a pocket. The Smith & Wesson factory was too busy during the war, however, to produce this model, so a subcontract was let to Savage and King of Middletown, Connecticut, for the major parts, and the completed pistols were introduced at the end of the war. In 1868 a further improvement was made, in appearance, and production continued until 1875.

Left: Smith & Wesson produced tip-up revolvers in three frame sizes: the Model 2 (top), Model 1½ (middle), and Model 1 (bottom). (Courtesy ArmchairGunShow.com.)

Right: The Model 1½ (bottom) was a compact five-shot version of the six-shot Model Two Old Army, which had enjoyed good popularity in the Civil War as a personal sidearm. Both were chambered for .32 rimfire cartridges. (Courtesy ArmchairGunShow.com.)

Model 2s at Auction

A major event in the collecting world was the Butterfield's auction in February 2001 of the John Otteman Collection of sixty-five Model 2 revolvers, many of them highly decorated or associated with historic figures. This collection had been assembled largely by previous owner Ronald H. Curtis, an outstanding expert in this field, who added a valuable technical discussion to the auction brochure.

Below: Cased engraved Model No. 2 Type IV Army revolver, serial no. 12487, .32in caliber with 6in barrel, nickel-plated with gold-washed hammer, cylinder and ejector. Extensive Nimschke-style scroll engraving; elephant ivory grips. (John Otteman Collection, courtesy Butterfields.)

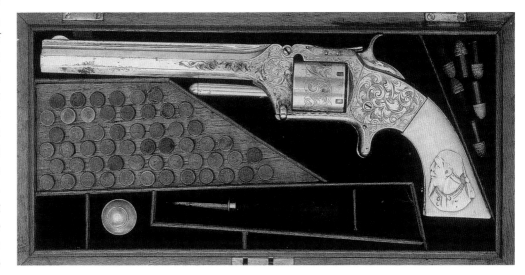

The auction catalog includes a guide to determining if the parts match, or if a pistol is made up of parts of different original guns. The same serial number as that shown on the butt should be repeated on the inside of one of the wood grips. Also, an assembly mark, which should match, was put on the face of the cylinder, the rear of the barrel, and on the front frame under the grip. These marks may be numbers, letters, or a combination of both.

Especially with highly decorated examples, there are rumors that altered or faked examples have come on the collectors' market (the author's observation, not from the Butterfield catalog).

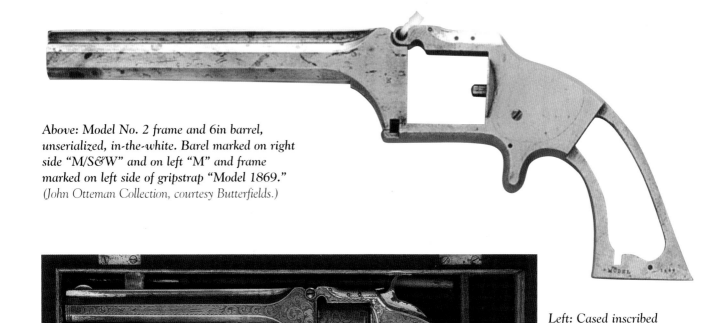

Above: Model No. 2 frame and 6in barrel, unserialized, in-the-white. Barel marked on right side "M/S&W" and on left "M" and frame marked on left side of gripstrap "Model 1869." (John Otteman Collection, courtesy Butterfields.)

Left: Cased inscribed and Nimschke-engraved Model No. 2 Type IV Army revolver, serial no. 17344, .32in caliber with 6in barrel. Gripstrap inscribed "O. F. Wisner/Capt. 22 N.Y.V.G." (John Otteman Collection, courtesy Butterfields.)

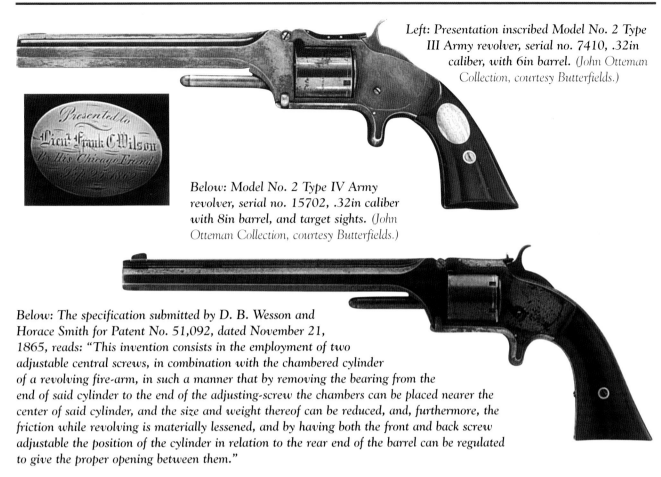

Left: Presentation inscribed Model No. 2 Type III Army revolver, serial no. 7410, .32in caliber, with 6in barrel. (John Otteman Collection, courtesy Butterfields.)

Below: Model No. 2 Type IV Army revolver, serial no. 15702, .32in caliber with 8in barrel, and target sights. (John Otteman Collection, courtesy Butterfields.)

Below: The specification submitted by D. B. Wesson and Horace Smith for Patent No. 51,092, dated November 21, 1865, reads: "This invention consists in the employment of two adjustable central screws, in combination with the chambered cylinder of a revolving fire-arm, in such a manner that by removing the bearing from the end of said cylinder to the end of the adjusting-screw the chambers can be placed nearer the center of said cylinder, and the size and weight thereof can be reduced, and, furthermore, the friction while revolving is materially lessened, and by having both the front and back screw adjustable the position of the cylinder in relation to the rear end of the barrel can be regulated to give the proper opening between them."

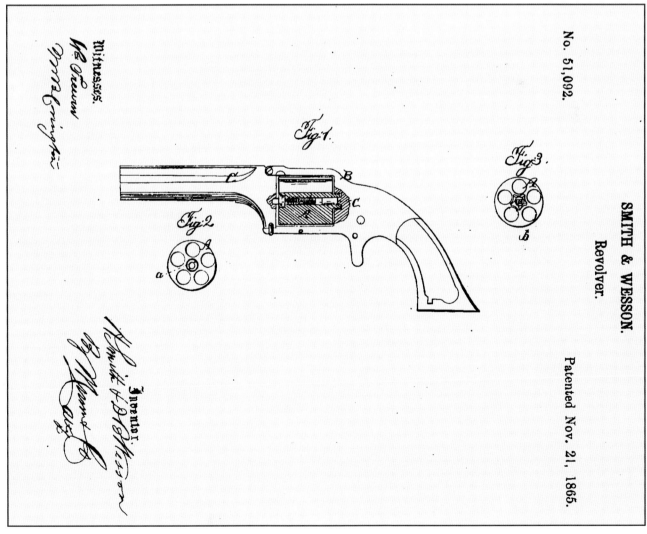

THE OLD WEST AND OVERSEAS

After the Civil War, half a million men went home with most of their guns, and the United States became the most heavily armed country in the world. Accordingly, the market for firearms manufacturers fell off drastically, and by 1867 Smith & Wesson was making only fifteen guns per month. Winchester and other manufacturers were similarly affected.

The answer to this problem was the superiority of American arms in the world market. Winchester was able to sell large numbers of its Model 1866 rifle to the French for the Franco-Prussian War, and also especially to Turkey, anticipating their war with Russia in 1877. Smith & Wesson attacked this world market vigorously at the Paris Exhibition of 1867, presenting highly decorated examples of its handguns and attracting the notice of Grand Duke Alexis of Russia, the son of the Czar. This laid the basis for large orders by the Russians starting in 1871, for a new large-caliber revolver suitable for military use (a counterpoint to the Winchester sales to Turkey; the Russians also ordered Berdan rifles from Colt's).

Smith & Wesson's first effort at a large caliber revolver was to arrange with Remington, on a royalty basis, to convert 4,575 of that company's .44in caliber New Model percussion revolvers to use a rimfire cartridge. Rollin White, however, objected to this, claiming that he had licensed his patent for the bored through cylinder only to Smith & Wesson itself. There was some suspicion that Smith & Wesson was trying to have the Rollin White patent extended, but in any event it was not, and by 1870 other companies were free to develop the cartridge revolvers. (Colt's had tried with limited success in the Thuer and Richardson conversions to use a cylinder loaded from the front with the firing pin connecting through an aperture at the rear.).

However, Smith & Wesson planned for this in advance and, as soon as the Rollin White patent expired in 1870, introduced a new pistol, using a top-break system in which the barrel folds down, a star-shaped plate automatically ejects the used cartridges, and fresh cartridges can quickly be

Above: A Russian Cossack, left, believed to be a bodyguard of a Kalmuck chieftain, carrying a .44in caliber Second Model Russian on a lanyard, with finger rest beneath the trigger guard being used to hold the revolver in the belt.

loaded. This formed the basis for a family of models extending up to after the turn of the century, with a total production of some 1,750,000 revolvers. The new design was a leap forward, as described in the Supica and Nahas *Standard Catalog of Smith & Wesson*: "Top-breaks were significantly sturdier designs than tip-ups, and were much faster to load and unload. Their chambering was primarily for the then-new center-fire calibers, which provided more

Right: Rufus Zogbaum's depiction of the defeat of Chief Roman Nose, in a stand by U.S. Cavalry Colonel Forsyth on the Arikara Fork of the Republican River in present-day Kansas, September 1868. (Courtesy Library of Congress.)

reliable ignition, reloadability, and more powerful rounds with less fear of tearing the rim."

The U.S. Ordnance Department was very interested in the new style revolver, since the settlement of the West was taking place. There were some 200,000 Native Americans of which some 50,000 were overtly hostile, and the Army had only 20,000 troops scattered along a series of frontier forts to maintain order. The Fetterman massacre of eighty troops near Fort Phil Kearney in Wyoming in 1866, the Wagon Box fight of August, 1867, and Colonel Forsyth's stand at the Arikara Fork in 1868 produced calls for breechloading repeating guns. In December 1870, Smith & Wesson delivered its first U.S. order of 1,000 Model 3 .44in caliber revolvers to the Springfield Armory (*note*: the model number for the tip-up and top-break revolvers refers only to frame size; there was a series of individual models within this overall classification).

MODEL 1½ AND MODEL 3 SINGLE ACTION TOP-BREAK REVOLVERS

Type and mechanical function: top-break, barrel pivots downward, with star-shaped ejector plate automatically coming out to extract used cartridges, then retracting when pivot reaches its maximum, allowing fresh cartridges to be inserted. Single action, hammer must be cocked by hand before each shot.

Models, caliber, and capacity: No. 1½, .32in caliber five-shot; .38in caliber Baby Russian, Mexican, and First to Third Models, five-shot; .44in caliber Russian and First to Third Models, six-shot; .45in caliber First and Second Model Schofield, six-shot.

Barrel lengths: .32in caliber, 3 to 10in; .38in caliber, 3½ to 10in; ,44in caliber, 6 to 8in; .45in caliber, 7in.

Manufactured: .32in, 1878-1872; .38in, 1876-1911; .44in, 1870-1912; .45in, 1875-1877.

Quantity: .32in, 97,574; .38in, approx. 137,000; .44in, approx. 250,820 (including Russian contract 131,138, and Schofield 8,969); .45in, 8,969.

Markings: Smith & Wesson, Springfield, MA, patent dates and serial numbers; special markings for U.S. Army, Russian and Japanese export, and Nashville Police.

Variations: different features with different models. The Second Model Russian has a substantially different appearance: a hump in the frame above the grip, itself a rounded "saw handle," and a curved finger grip extension below the trigger guard.

Above: A Russian officer with Smith & Wesson revolver drawn (note lanyard) towers over people begging for bread at the mayor's house near Simbirsk, in R. Caton Woodville's 1892 depiction of famine in Russia. (Courtesy Library of Congress.)

The Russian government, already impressed with Smith & Wesson's tip-up revolvers as related above, welcomed the new large caliber revolver for its military, and ordered a total of over 131,000 of this model, modified to use the .44in S&W Russian. This placed the company on a permanent basis as a major world wide arms manufacturer. Another result of the new revolver, with the purchase of 1,000 by the U.S. Army, was attracting the interest of Major George W. Schofield, a member of the 10th Cavalry, whose brother John was president of the Small Arms Board. George Schofield was so impressed that he asked to be an agent

Above: Model 3 Army "Russian," which used a special .44in caliber cartridge specified by the Russian Army. When Smith & Wesson won the order from Russia, it had to devote almost its entire capacity for five years to delivering over 131,000 of the weapons.

Above: The New Model 3 Russian, also in .44in caliber, incorporated changes from the previous weapon, including, for instance, the absence of the finger spur.

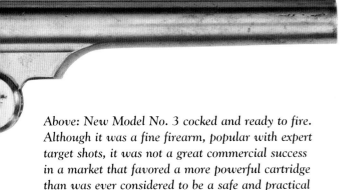

Above: New Model No. 3 cocked and ready to fire. Although it was a fine firearm, popular with expert target shots, it was not a great commercial success in a market that favored a more powerful cartridge than was ever considered to be a safe and practical proposition in a break-open arm; generally, solid-frame revolvers were preferred.

Above: Major George W. Schofield, U.S. Army, who proposed and on June 2, 1871, patented improvements to Smith & Wesson's Model 3 single action top-break revolver.

selling these arms in the West, and also proposed an improvement to make it more usable for the cavalry.

The major feature of this improvement, for which Schofield obtained parts from the company to build a model and then took out a patent, was to move the latch which allowed the barrel to fold to the frame instead of the top strap. This allowed the user to release the barrel with the thumb of the same hand holding the revolver, so that a rider could reload while maintaining control of his horse. The improved model, called the Schofield, was produced in the .45in caliber required by the Army.

By this time Colt's had developed its own .45in caliber

Single Action Army, the "Peacemaker," and the Army held trials in 1873 to compare this with Smith & Wesson's Schofield model. The Colt won, being regarded as simpler and sturdier, and it was also less expensive; but the Schofield was still not out of the picture. Additional Schofields were ordered by the Army, but there was a problem: the Schofield would take a shorter version of the .45in Colt cartridge only, while the Colt pistol would take both versions, and the

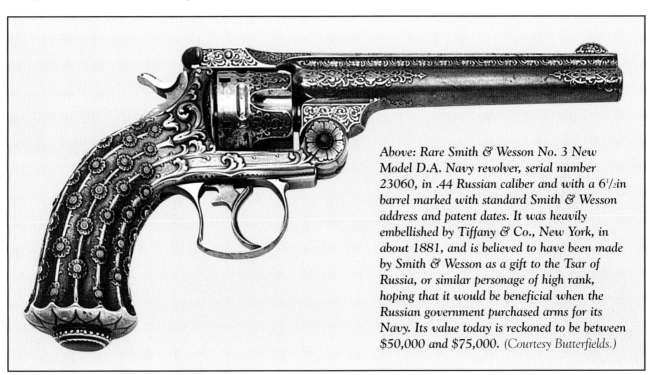

Above: Rare Smith & Wesson No. 3 New Model D.A. Navy revolver, serial number 23060, in .44 Russian caliber and with a 6½in barrel marked with standard Smith & Wesson address and patent dates. It was heavily embellished by Tiffany & Co., New York, in about 1881, and is believed to have been made by Smith & Wesson as a gift to the Tsar of Russia, or similar personage of high rank, hoping that it would be beneficial when the Russian government purchased arms for its Navy. Its value today is reckoned to be between $50,000 and $75,000. (Courtesy Butterfields.)

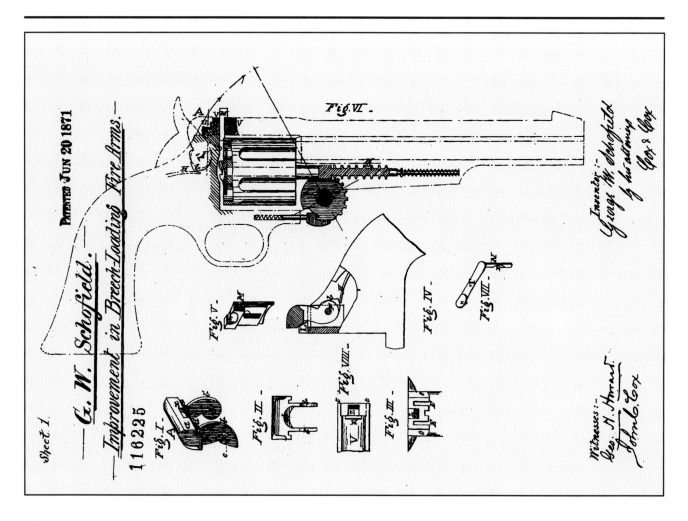

Above: Some of the drawings supporting Col. George W. Schofield's Patent No. 116,225, the objectives of which, according to Scholfield's specification statement, were, "...first, to provide a lock-fast for such weapons [which open for loading by turning on a pivot, which pivot connects the barrel and the frame], which shall hold the barrel securely in the position for firing; second, to provide a cylinder-stay for holding the cylinder in position when the weapon was opened for loading or ejecting discharged cartridge-cases; third, to provide a simple and effective ejector-spring stop."

wrong cartridge was issued to one of the frontier posts for their Schofields. This may have contributed to the end of this model in 1880, or Smith & Wesson itself may have lost interest, having come up with a newer model. Some observers commented that Custer might have had more of a chance with it in the Seventh Cavalry massacre of 1876. Discouraged by his gun's failure and also the death of his wife, Major Schofield committed suicide in 1883.

The Smith & Wesson Model 3, in the version sold in the U.S. as the First Model American, was the first large caliber

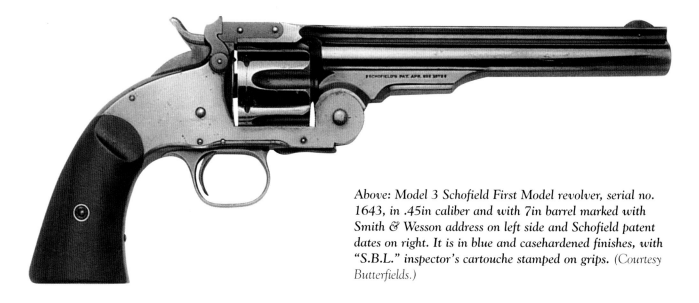

Above: Model 3 Schofield First Model revolver, serial no. 1643, in .45in caliber and with 7in barrel marked with Smith & Wesson address on left side and Schofield patent dates on right. It is in blue and casehardened finishes, with "S.B.L." inspector's cartouche stamped on grips. (Courtesy Butterfields.)

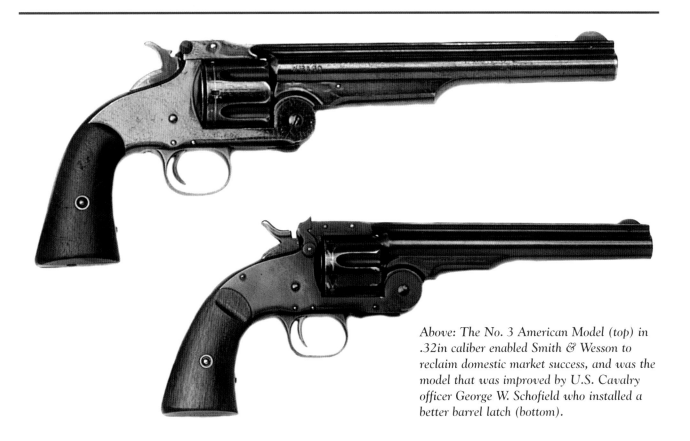

Above: The No. 3 American Model (top) in
.32in caliber enabled Smith & Wesson to
reclaim domestic market success, and was the
model that was improved by U.S. Cavalry
officer George W. Schofield who installed a
better barrel latch (bottom).

Right: It was not just for its innovative firearms designs
that the Smith & Wesson company came to the attention of
the press, but also for its commercial success assisted by
advanced machinery and mass-production techniques (as
evidenced by this front cover of Scientific American,
January 24, 1880).

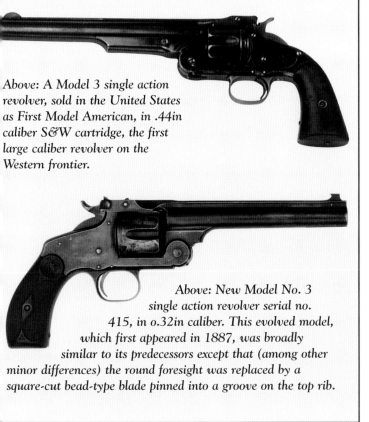

Above: A Model 3 single action
revolver, sold in the United States
as First Model American, in .44in
caliber S&W cartridge, the first
large caliber revolver on the
Western frontier.

Above: New Model No. 3
single action revolver serial no.
415, in o.32in caliber. This evolved model,
which first appeared in 1887, was broadly
similar to its predecessors except that (among other
minor differences) the round foresight was replaced by a
square-cut bead-type blade pinned into a groove on the top rib.

Above: Lt. Col. George Armstrong Custer in a reclined pose with Grand Duke Alexis (Alexei Aleksandrovich) of Russia prior to their buffalo hunting trip. It is possible that the Grand Duke is holding in his right hand the revolver presented to him during his visit to the Smith & Wesson factory in December 1871. According to the Springfield Daily Republican at the time, the firearm was "an elegant pistol, inlaid with gold, having pearl butt upon which were the coat of arms of America and Russia, and inclosed into a rosewood case, bearing the inscription 'From S&W to A.A.'" (Courtesy Library of Congress.)

revolver on the Western frontier, and it had a distinguished record. Grand Duke Alexis of Russia visited the Smith & Wesson factory in 1871, after which he went on a hunting trip to the West accompanied by George Custer and "Buffalo Bill" Cody, and killed a buffalo at 30 yards with one of the company's revolvers. This was a momentous trip, in that Cody had Native Americans perform as entertainers, laying the basis for his later Wild West shows, while Custer's taking the group into the Dakota Badlands, which the Native

Right: A .45in caliber Smith & Wesson Schofield takes pride of place (below center) in an array of weapons attributed to Jesse James and apparently authenticated by his son. The label inscription reads: "Schofield. One of the guns Jesse James took of and laid on the bed just before he was assassinated by Bob Ford." (Courtesy Library of Congress.)

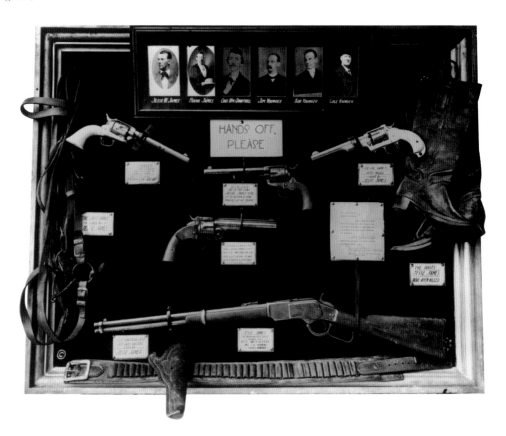

Right: Famous users of First Model Americans included (center) "Buffalo Bill" Cody and "Texas Jack" Omohundro (right). At left is Edward Judsen, alias "Ned Buntline," notorious drunk whose own life would have made an ideal subject for his prolific output of dime novel yarns.

Americans considered sacred, may have contributed to the uprising which led to the Little Bighorn massacre. First Model Americans or Schofields were carried by Cody himself and his partner "Texas Jack" Omohundro, and by Marshals Dallas Stoudenmire and Bill Tilghman, as well as apparently Wyatt Earp at the O.K. Corral. On the other side of the law, No. 3s were carried by the famous train robbers Jesse and Frank James and by Cole Younger, who with his brothers sometimes accompanied the James's in train and bank robberies. Younger also gave one of these pistols to Belle Starr, the "Bandit Queen," who bore his illegitimate child.

The Model 2 single action top-break, in .38in caliber, was popularly known as the Baby Russian, because of its similarity to the .44in caliber Model 3 sold to the Russian military. It also had substantial sales, even though it was not ordered by the Russians. At first it had only a spur trigger, but starting in 1881 was fitted with a regular trigger-guard. With its small frame, it was popular in the Old West for concealment, after marshals prohibited the carrying of pistols in exposed holsters in towns. Another claim to fame for this model was the company's introduction of the new .38in centerfire cartridge that was one of the most popular revolver cartridges made, and is still made today as the .38 Smith & Wesson.

Top-break double action revolvers

Smith & Wesson began experimenting with double action revolvers in 1872, and the Russian Government had the company design a model which, however, it did not accept. The British, with the Adams revolver, had developed this system as far back as 1851, modified in 1885 to allow both double and single action as in present day revolvers, although there were problems in using it with the percussion cap and ball system. Mechanically, there is not a great deal of difference between single and double action. For the latter, a strut is added to connect the trigger movement to the hammer. There are the disadvantages of more parts than in a single action and in a harder trigger pull, but the advantage is a faster action since the hammer does not have to be pulled back by hand.

Smith & Wesson began producing double action revolvers in 1880, after Colt's introduction of its double action Lightning in 1877. D. B. Wesson had been reluctant to release the double action revolver until it was perfected, but noted that sales of single action revolvers were falling off

Above: Smith & Wesson's double action 1881 Frontier revolver in .44in caliber never could compete successfully with Colt's double action Lightning, introduced in 1877.

Above: Smith & Wesson's First Model top-break double action style was to become replaced by the solid frame designs from 1899.

(No Model.)

No. 401,087.

D. B. WESSON.
REVOLVING FIRE ARM.

Patented Apr. 9, 1889.

Above: According to the specifications related to Daniel B. Wesson's Patent No. 401,087 dated April 9, 1889, the objective of his invention was "an improvement in fire-arms, and particularly to the notches in the sides of the cylinders thereof, the purpose thereof being to render the walls of said notches more enduring resulting in the increased efficiency of the cylinder."

after Colt introduced its double action arm. A series of variations were produced until well after the turn of the century, although the top-break double action revolver was rapidly replaced after 1899 by the next major development, the solid frame "Hand Ejector" design with a swing-out cylinder. It is interesting to note that the final modification

Above and right: Smith & Wesson's Safety Hammerless models (top, First Model, and bottom, Third Model) were small and compact and designed as pocket revolvers in which reliability and reasonable stopping power were more important than long-range accuracy.

of the .38in top-break revolver, introduced in 1903, was to make most of its parts interchangeable with the swing-out cylinder revolvers, thus reducing production costs.

The double action revolver was understandably popular with gunfighters in the West. It was preferred by William "Billy the Kid" Bonney, who owned a Smith & Wesson as well as a Colt; and by the equally famous (at the time) multiple killer, John Wesley Hardin. However, production did not reach nearly the level of the earlier single action revolvers because the Russian military was not interested in it, in spite of the company's efforts.

There was a special series of top-break double action revolvers, called the Safety Hammerless, in which the hammer was concealed inside the frame. There is an unsubstantiated story that D. B. Wesson developed this model after hearing of a child being hurt accidentally by playing with one of the double action models. In any event,

he and his son Joe added two more safety features: a lever on the back of the handle that had to be pressed before the revolver would fire, and internal construction such that the firing pin would not set off the cartridge unless the hammer was released by the trigger. The hammerless design also made it easier for the pistol to be drawn from a coat pocket, since there was no outside hammer to be caught on clothing. An updated version of this same design is made today. The grip safety feature also led to the pistol being called the "Lemon Squeezer." This same feature is incorporated in many later pistols, such as the Colt .45 automatic.

Supica and Nahas note in their *Standard Catalog of Smith & Wesson* that many other firms copied the top-break design, especially the .32in and .38in Double Action and Hammerless models, producing millions in the late 1800s and early 1900s. Harrington & Richardson and Iver Johnson were two of the largest manufacturers. Their products varied in

Above: A well-used example of the New Model double action .38in revolver. The left side of the frame has an access plate so that the mechanism could be reached, while the unsightly brass screw visible on the right side of this weapon jammed into its aperture, and is due to be replaced!

TOP-BREAK DOUBLE ACTION REVOLVERS

Type and mechanical function: top-break, barrel pivots downward, with star-shaped ejector plate automatically coming out to extract used cartridges, then retracting when pivot reaches its maximum, allowing fresh cartridges to be inserted. Double action, pulling the trigger cocks the hammer for each shot; some models can also be used in single action by cocking the hammer by hand.

Models, caliber, and capacity: ,32in caliber, First to Fifth Models with exterior hammer, also First to Third Model Safety Hammerless ("Lemon Squeezer") with interior hammer, five-shot; .38in caliber, First to Fifth and Perfected Models, First to Fifth Safety Hammerless Models, five-shot; .44in caliber, First Model and Wesson Favorite, six-shot.

Barrel length: .32in caliber, 3 to 10in; .38in caliber 3¼ to 6in; .44in caliber, 4 to 6½in.

Manufactured: .32in, 1880-1937; .38in, 1880-1940; .44in, 1870-1883.

Quantity: .32in, 330,962; .38in, approx. 874,875; .44in, 54,590.

Markings: Smith & Wesson, Springfield, MA, patent dates and serial numbers.

Variations: different features with different models.

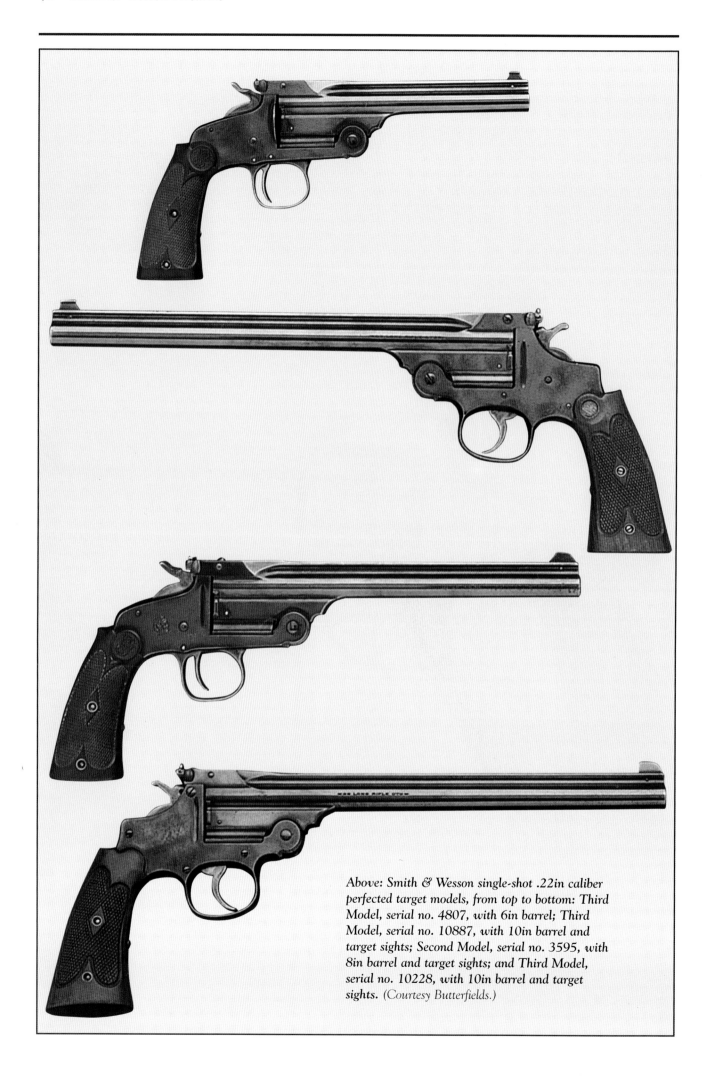

Above: Smith & Wesson single-shot .22in caliber perfected target models, from top to bottom: Third Model, serial no. 4807, with 6in barrel; Third Model, serial no. 10887, with 10in barrel and target sights; Second Model, serial no. 3595, with 8in barrel and target sights; and Third Model, serial no. 10228, with 10in barrel and target sights. (Courtesy Butterfields.)

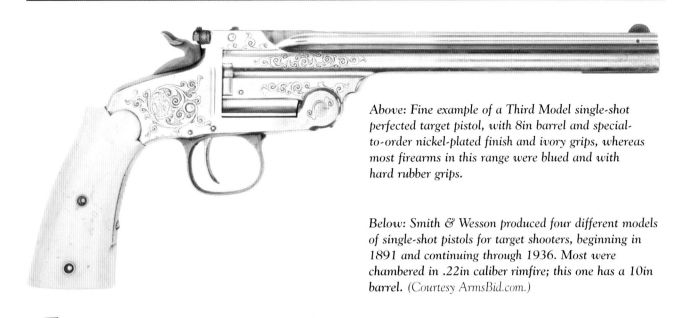

Above: Fine example of a Third Model single-shot perfected target pistol, with 8in barrel and special-to-order nickel-plated finish and ivory grips, whereas most firearms in this range were blued and with hard rubber grips.

Below: Smith & Wesson produced four different models of single-shot pistols for target shooters, beginning in 1891 and continuing through 1936. Most were chambered in .22in caliber rimfire; this one has a 10in barrel. (Courtesy ArmsBid.com.)

their details from the Smith & Wesson models, of course, but the companies took advantage of the company's pioneering concept.

Another category of top-break pistols made by Smith & Wesson were the single-shot target models. The First Model, also known as the Model of 1891, was made from about 1893 to 1905, in .22in, .32in, and .38in calibers, with a revolver-type frame complete with semicircular recoil shields behind the cylinder. The Second Model, made from 1905 to 1909, was only in .22in caliber, and omitted the recoil shields. The Third Model, called the Perfected Target Pistol, was made from about 1909 to 1923. Total production of the three models was 13,115. A Fourth Model, not top-break but resembling a

Left: A Smith & Wesson advertisement, circa 1898-1910. Competition at the time was intense, but Smith & Wesson's reputation was good, its products finely made and reliable in operation, and its marketing was well-targeted. (Courtesy Smith & Wesson.)

Above and below: There were only 977 of the Model 320 revolving rifle made, based closely on the No. 3 revolver, but with a two-piece barrel screwed together about 2in in front of the breech. There were three barrel lengths, 16in, 18in (as both here), and 20in. Both rifles shown have 18in barrels and blued foresights on the top rib and an L-shaped backsight; on the weapon at top an aperture backsight, an optional extra, may be seen on the clamp which holds the rifle butt onto the revolver. (Bottom photo courtesy Butterfields.)

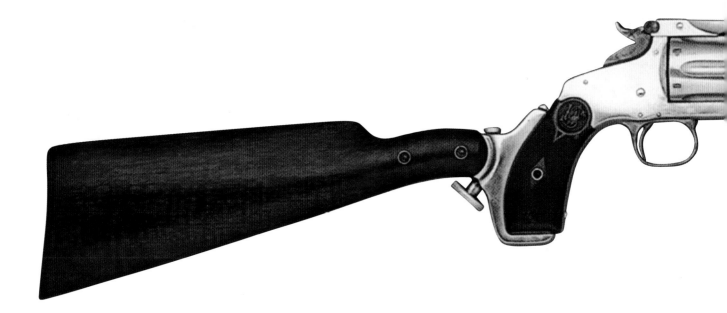

modern semiautomatic, was made from about 1925 to 1936, with production of 1,870. All these models reflect the company's continuing interest in precision manufacturing and the shooting sports. Special versions of revolvers were also designed for target shooting; the No. 3 black powder revolver was said to dominate the matches at England's famous Bisley range.

Still another variation of the top-break revolver was the Model 320 revolving rifle using a .320 cartridge, with 977 made between 1879 and 1887. This used a pistol frame with a barrel up to 20in long and a detachable shoulder stock. Its popularity was limited by the shooter's hand forward of the cylinder being subject to peppering by particles escaping from the cylinder.

Horace Smith remained an active partner in the company until 1873, when he retired at the age of 65. Remarkably, and reflecting the long and amicable relationship between the two partners, Smith sold his entire interest in the company to D. B. Wesson for only $200,000 payable over five years, a very small sum in view of the partners' $165,000 salaries in 1865. D.B.'s three sons, Joe, Walter, and Frank, who died in 1887, all played an active role in the business. The company enjoyed great prosperity through the turn of the century, concentrating on the production of revolvers with only a short detour into the production of sewing machines in 1880.

Right: The venerable Daniel B. Wesson with two of his sons, Joseph H. standing, and Walter H. seated at left. (Courtesy Connecticut Valley Historical Museum.)

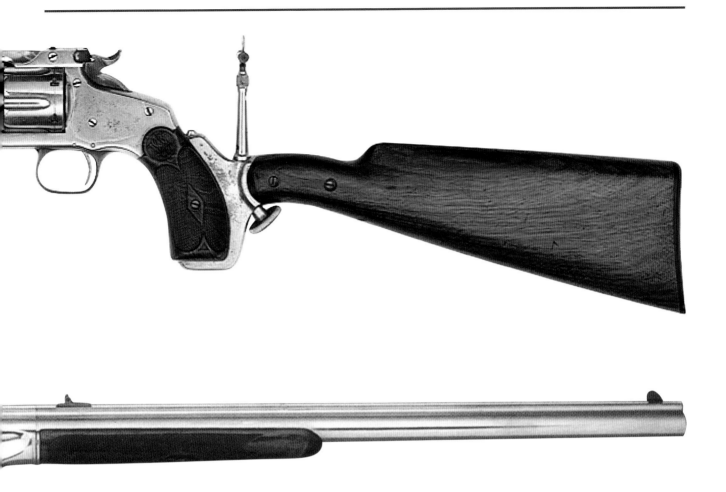

THE SWING-OUT CYLINDER
AND .38 SPECIAL

The next great advance in revolver design, after the tip-up (with a self-contained cartridge) and the top-break with automatic ejection, was the solid frame with the swing-out cylinder. Colt's pioneered this in 1889 and Smith & Wesson followed it up in 1896. Ironically, Smith & Wesson called this its "Hand Ejector" revolver, a name which suggests incorrectly that it was less advanced than the top-break with its automatic ejection.

Actually, the swing-out cylinder revolver is stronger, with a solid frame, and easier to use because it can stay aligned in the direction of the target while it is being loaded and unloaded. Ejection is carried out simply by pushing a rod in front of the cylinder which activates the same kind of star-shaped ejector as in the top-break system. This is easy to do and, using the latch provided on the left side of the gun to allow the cylinder to swing out (or in early models pulling a rod under the barrel), is simpler than opening a latch on the frame to allow the barrel to pivot, as in the top-break models.

The major Smith & Wesson "Hand Ejector" models made from their beginning around 1900 up to the start of World War II are described in the accompanying specifications panels. A word about the company's complicated system of nomenclature is appropriate here. Until the introduction of Hand Ejectors, there were only officially three models: No.1 and 1½, .22in caliber; No. 2, .32in caliber; and No.3 .44in and .34in calibers. After the Hand Ejectors were introduced, each caliber was given a name, such as Ladysmith and Military and Police, with model numbers within them; that is, up to 1957, when numbers were given to each of the many models being offered in the company's greatly expanded catalogs. There is also a system of letters for frame sizes which is not always easy to decipher: M refers to the small early Ladysmith frame, I to the small .32 frame, J to the small .38 frame, K to the medium .38 frame, I to medium large, and N to the largest .44 Magnum type frame.

The first Hand Ejector model was in .32in caliber,

Above: The .32 Hand Ejector First Model, introduced in 1896, was the first S&W revolver with a swing-out cylinder. Unique features abandoned on subsequent models included the placement of the company and patent markings on the cylinder, and a cylinder stop integral with the rear sight on the topstrap of the frame (a throw-back last found on the early tip-up models). (Courtesy ArmchairGunShow.com.)

introduced in 1896. A significant improvement was made in 1903 by providing a thumb latch on the left side of the frame to release the cylinder. There was immediate interest by police departments, with early orders from Jersey City and Philadelphia. The .32 S&W Long cartridge was introduced, a half-inch longer than the regular .32 S&W for greater power. Although eventually eclipsed for police use by the .38in caliber models, a variation with a square butt was called the .32 Regulation Police and was made from 1917 to 1942, and the overall appearance of this model stayed unchanged until well after World War II.

The frame size of the .32in model was also adapted for .22in revolvers. This was called the Bekeart after a San Francisco gun dealer, Philip Bekeart, who urged this change

from the small frame Ladysmith and made a commitment to buy 1,000 himself. After the original issue, the model was just called the .22/32, and it was also made in a popular variation called the Kit Gun with a 4in barrel, designed to be carried on hunting and fishing trips.

Below: S&W .22 Hand Ejector revolvers have included the I frame 22/32 Hand Ejector (top) introduced as the Bekeart Model in 1911, tiny M frame Ladysmith .22 Hand Ejectors (middle) produced from 1902 to 1921, and K frame 22s such as the K-22 Masterpiece (bottom) with successor models such as the Model 617 continued through today. Kit Gun .22s built on the I and J frames (not pictured) have also enjoyed great popularity. (Courtesy ArmchairGunShow.com)

.22 LADYSMITH AND BEKEART .22/32 HAND EJECTOR TO 1941

Type: hand ejector swing-out cylinder; Ladysmith with small M frame, Bekeart with medium I frame as in .32in models.

Capacity: Ladysmith seven-shot revolver, Bekeart six-shot..

Barrel lengths: 2¹/₂ to 6in.

Manufactured: Ladysmith 1902 to 1921; Bekeart 1911 to 1953.

Quantity: Ladysmith 26,154; Bekeart, original as ordered by Bekeart, 1,000, rest several hundred thousand, target model.

Variations: First Model Ladysmith had latch to swing cylinder out on side, Second and Third Models used an attachment to the ejector rod. The Bekeart, with a larger frame, used the side latch.

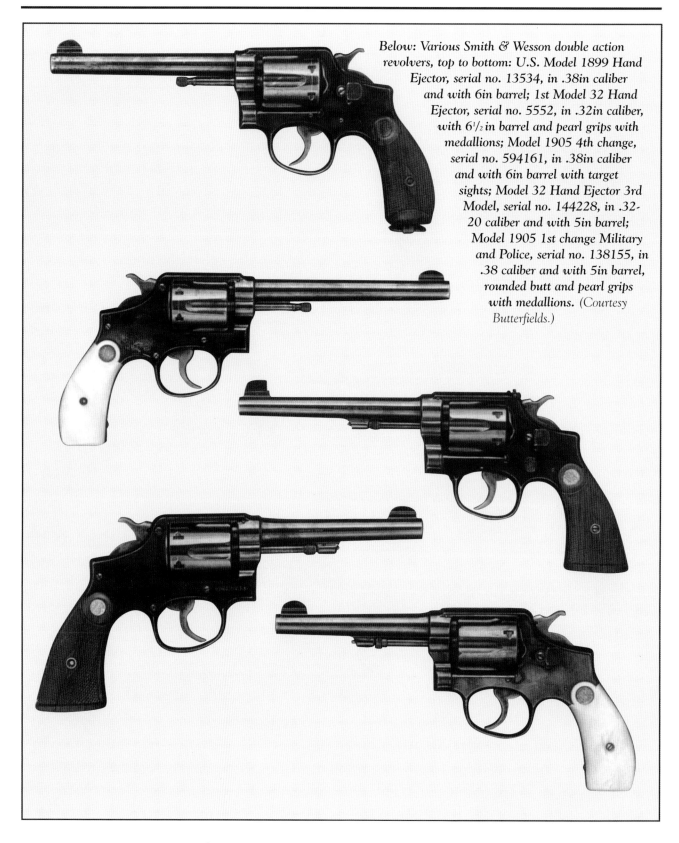

Below: Various Smith & Wesson double action revolvers, top to bottom: U.S. Model 1899 Hand Ejector, serial no. 13534, in .38in caliber and with 6in barrel; 1st Model 32 Hand Ejector, serial no. 5552, in .32in caliber, with 6½ in barrel and pearl grips with medallions; Model 1905 4th change, serial no. 594161, in .38in caliber and with 6in barrel with target sights; Model 32 Hand Ejector 3rd Model, serial no. 144228, in .32-20 caliber and with 5in barrel; Model 1905 1st change Military and Police, serial no. 138155, in .38 caliber and with 5in barrel, rounded butt and pearl grips with medallions. (Courtesy Butterfields.)

The early version of the .22in Hand Ejector, the Ladysmith, was diminutive in size, and is particularly attractive for present day collectors. The name is still used by the company for some of its smaller sized revolvers to emphasize their use by women for self-defense, but spelled LadySmith. There is an entertaining but probably fictional story that the conservative D. B. Wesson ordered discontinuation of the production of the first model when he learned that it had acquired a reputation among the "ladies of the evening" of the time; actually, he died in 1906, while production of the small Ladysmith continued until 1921.

The .38in Military and Police Model 10 has historically been the mainstay of the Smith & Wesson Company, with some 6,000,000 of this general type produced to date. It has been described as the most successful handgun of all time, and the most popular centerfire revolver of the 20th Century. Noted gun writer Paul Scarlata points out, in the magazine Smith and Wesson Handguns 2002, that essentially

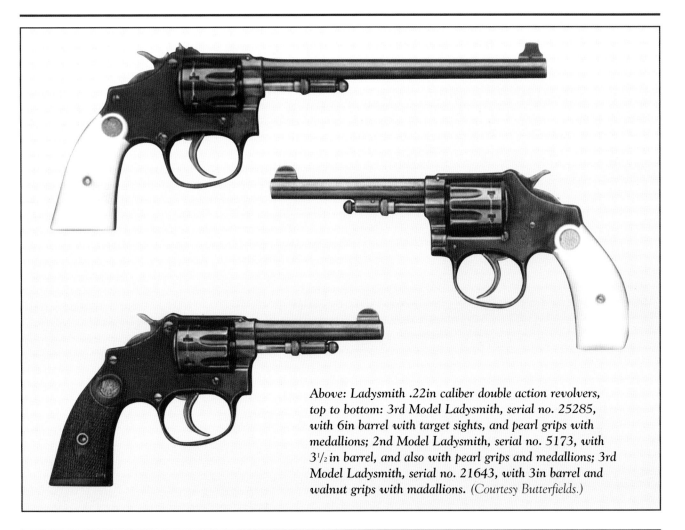

Above: Ladysmith .22in caliber double action revolvers, top to bottom: 3rd Model Ladysmith, serial no. 25285, with 6in barrel with target sights, and pearl grips with medallions; 2nd Model Ladysmith, serial no. 5173, with 3¹/₂in barrel, and also with pearl grips and medallions; 3rd Model Ladysmith, serial no. 21643, with 3in barrel and walnut grips with madallions. (Courtesy Butterfields.)

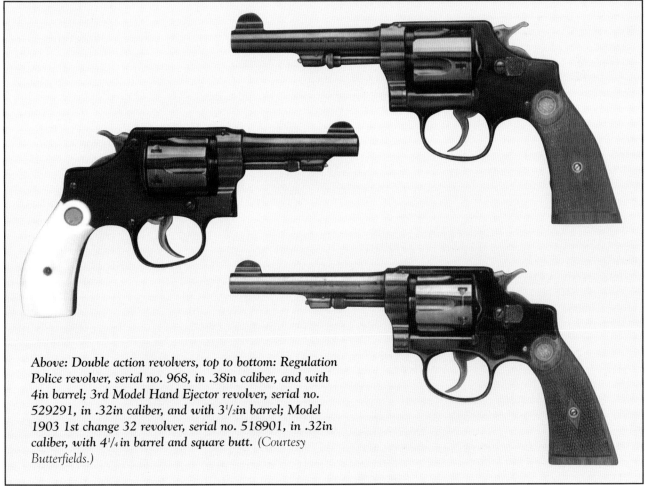

Above: Double action revolvers, top to bottom: Regulation Police revolver, serial no. 968, in .38in caliber, and with 4in barrel; 3rd Model Hand Ejector revolver, serial no. 529291, in .32in caliber, and with 3¹/₂in barrel; Model 1903 1st change 32 revolver, serial no. 518901, in .32in caliber, with 4¹/₄in barrel and square butt. (Courtesy Butterfields.)

Catalogue of Latest Models for Stamp
SMITH & WESSON
10 Stockbridge Street   Springfield, Mass.

Left: As the 20th century dawned, the Smith & Wesson company was aggressively looking for overseas business to go along with its Turkish export sales, and dramatic earlier Russian orders. The company proudly announced that soon-to-be Russia's enemy, Japan, had chosen S&W firearms for its Navy.

unchanged versions of the gun are still being offered by the company today, and he describes its popularity as follows:

"By the 1930s the Military and Police was being used by a large percentage of the police agencies in the Western Hemisphere and was equally popular with civilian shooters. The reason for its renown was simple: the medium sized K-Frame proved to be the right size for the average person's hand, permitting it to handle the recoil of the .38 Special cartridge with aplomb. It came about as close to a 'one size fits all' handgun as could be wished for . . . Combined with S&W's reputation for quality and durability, the Military and Police became the standard by which all other medium-frame revolvers were judged."

The longevity of the cartridge introduced in 1899 for the Military and Police model is as impressive as that of the gun's design. The .38 S&W Special cartridge was completely redesigned, with substantially greater power, from the .38in round used for the top-break Baby Russian. It is not interchangeable with this earlier cartridge, which is called

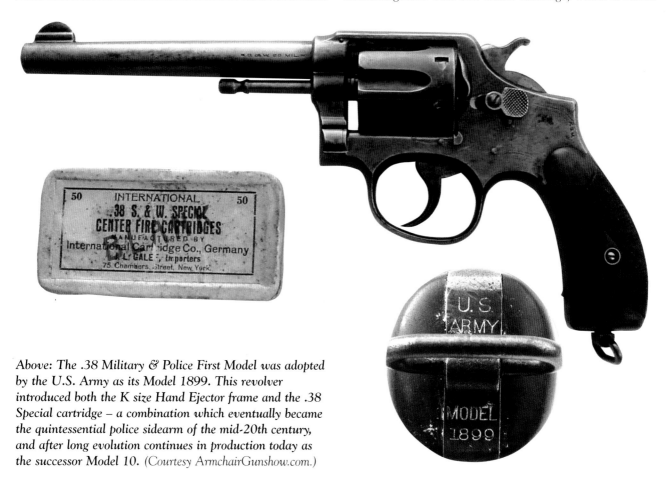

Above: The .38 Military & Police First Model was adopted by the U.S. Army as its Model 1899. This revolver introduced both the K size Hand Ejector frame and the .38 Special cartridge – a combination which eventually became the quintessential police sidearm of the mid-20th century, and after long evolution continues in production today as the successor Model 10. (Courtesy ArmchairGunshow.com.)

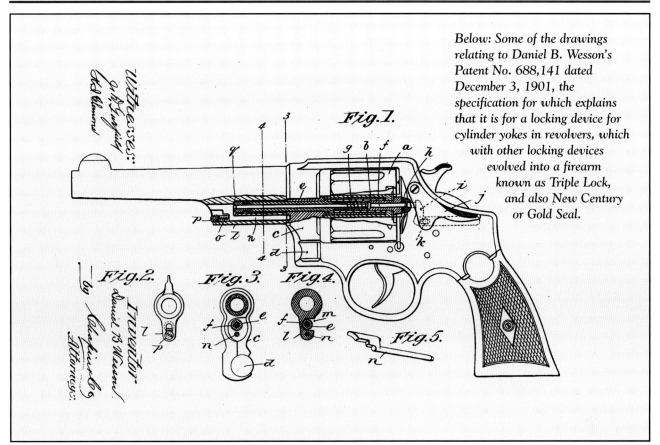

Below: Some of the drawings relating to Daniel B. Wesson's Patent No. 688,141 dated December 3, 1901, the specification for which explains that it is for a locking device for cylinder yokes in revolvers, which with other locking devices evolved into a firearm known as Triple Lock, and also New Century or Gold Seal.

Above and right: A .38 Military & Police with frame cut away and clear sideplate installed to show mechanical operation. (Courtesy Old Town Station Dispatch.)

the .38 S&W, and is dangerous to use in the earlier model gun. The success of the .38 S&W Special cartridge is evidenced by the millions of revolvers, many closely copying the design of the Military and Police, which have been made by other companies around the world.

The .44in caliber Hand Ejector model produced more modest sales for the company, but established a reputation for power and reliability which helped form the foundation for the company's spectacularly successful .44in Magnum in 1955. The first version of this model, which was introduced in 1908 as part of a

.38 CALIBER HAND EJECTOR MILITARY AND POLICE MODELS TO 1942

Type: hand ejector swing-out cylinder, K frame.

Capacity: six-shot revolver.

Barrel lengths: 2 to 6½in.

Manufactured: 1899 to 1942.

Quantity: 671,349.

Variations: First Model 1899-1902, Second Model 1902-1942, with four changes.

Above: The 2nd Model .44 Hand Ejector (top, in scarce adjustable sight Target Model configuration) eliminated the ejector shroud and 3rd locking lug of the 1st Model "Triple Lock." The 3rd Model .44 HE (bottom) brought back the shroud to protect the rod from bending. Many 3rd Models were sold through one Texas distributor, leading to its nickname as the "Wolf & Klar Model." (Courtesy ArmchairGunShow.com.)

Above: A New Century revolver serial no. 1068, of the type that was sold to the British Army in some quantity. It has a British number on the bottom of the butt strap, together with London proof marks. This model was sometimes also called "0.44 Hand Ejector First Model," the "Gold Seal," or the "Triple Lock."

.44 HAND EJECTOR MODEL

Type: hand ejector swing-out cylinder with release latch on frame.

Capacity: six-shot revolver.

Barrel lengths: 4 to 6½in.

Made: 1908 to 1941.

Quantity: 83,053.

Variations: First Model, made in 1908-1915, known as the Triple Lock.

Above and left: Daniel B. Wesson's sons Walter H. (left) and Joseph H. became equal partners on his death on 1906, and they alternated as company president for some time. But management problems arose, such that the U.S. Army had to take over control in 1918 to make sure of wartime production.

planned schedule of release of Hand Ejectors of different calibers, had an extra feature which has the nickname of the "Triple Lock." As well as the cylinder being anchored by the center pin extending into the back of the frame and a lug coming up through the bottom, it was also held by a lug in the yoke in front of the cylinder, and also the ejector rod was housed in a shroud. The extra front lock proved expensive, however, and was dropped with the Second Model of 1915. In 1926 the distributors Wolf and Klar of Fort Worth, Texas, asked for a new version of the shrouded extractor rod, and 1,000 of this variation was shipped to them. Examples with the Wolf and Klar markings are prized by collectors.

D. B. Wesson died in 1906. His tenure as president had been long. He had run the company with a firm hand, making the major decisions and also taking part in the design of the company's new revolver models. His two sons, Walter and Joe, were equal partners, with Walter serving as office manager and treasurer and Joe as chief designer and general supervisor. While Walter became the president after D.B.'s death, there was apparently no agreement on the direction the company should take. A trusteeship was set up to control the company in 1912, but with Walter and Joe alternating as president, and with each in failing health, the company was not able to organize itself for the large influx of military orders at the beginning of America's military involvement in World War I in 1917. In 1918, therefore, the U.S. Army assumed the management of the plant for the short period of time until the war ended.

Military Smith & Wessons

The Colt company stole a march on Smith & Wesson in regard to military orders for the swingout cylinder revolver, first introducing its New Model Navy model in 1889 and the New Model Army shortly afterward, using the .38in Long Colt cartridge. Military purchases of Smith & Wesson revolvers did not take place until 1901, when the Navy and the Army respectively ordered 1,000 each of the Military and Police model, using the Long Colt cartridge. After that, however, this model, with its improved .38 Special cartridge, was used in large quantities by the military.

Many Smith & Wesson revolvers were purchased privately by officers and enlisted men before these were officially adopted by the services. A spectacular example is Theodore Roosevelt, as related by Phil Schreier of the National Firearms Museum. TR was Secretary of the Navy at the time the battleship USS *Maine* blew up in Havana Harbor in Cuba on February 15, 1898, signaling the start of the Spanish-American War. He promptly resigned his position, took a commission in the Army, and left for Texas to help Colonel Leonard Wood form the volunteer cavalry unit that became known as Roosevelt's Rough Riders. At the same time he ordered a pair of engraved New Model American Smith & Wesson revolvers, which arrived at his home in Sagamore Hill on Long Island, New York, the day

Above: After extensive practice the American Expeditionary Forces revolver team ultimately selected the Smith & Wesson .38in Military & Police revolver as its choice for its competitive events at the Interallied Games, where the team won the International Team match, the first 8 places and 19 of the first 21 prizes in the Interallied Individual Pistol match. (Courtesy National Archives.)

before he left for Cuba.

The next war action engaged in by the U.S. military was the Philippine Insurrection, which lasted from 1899 to 1901, after the islands were acquired by the United States as a result of the Spanish-American War. Here it was found that the .38in caliber revolver did not have the power to stop crazed "insurrectos" swinging bolo knives. Again Smith & Wesson was bypassed; the Army ordered 4,600 Colt Model 1878 Frontier revolvers in .45in caliber with enlarged trigger guards (known mistakenly as the Alaska model), and then started purchasing Colt's new semiautomatic pistol invented by John Browning, which started as the Model 1900 and culminated in the hugely successful .45in caliber Model 1911.

With the start of World War I in Europe in 1914, military orders finally came to the fore, reviving Smith & Wesson's somewhat stagnant market. Just before the war began, the British government wrote the company president Walter Wesson asking for a new revolver in .45in caliber that would use the British .45 Mark II cartridge. Production of this revolver began immediately, first with the triple lock system and then without, and by September 1916, a total of 74,755 had been made for the British Commonwealth countries.

With the involvement of the United States in the war in Europe appearing likely, Smith & Wesson worked with the Springfield Armory to develop a similar revolver using the .45in ACP cartridge used for the Colt Model 1911 automatic. Known as the 1917 .45 Hand Ejector U.S. Service Model, this massive revolver had the distinguishing feature of loading its cartridges with semicircular "half moon" clips, with three cartridges at a time inserted at their base. This was necessary because the .45 ACP cartridge does not have a protruding rim which would be caught by the star-shaped extractor at the rear of the gun's cylinder.

The importance of this model in the war effort of World War I is illustrated by its total production of 163,476 in only the two years in which the United States was in the war. While the Colt automatic was the primary military sidearm, not enough of these weapons could be manufactured; the Colt company also made its New Service revolver in .45 caliber, producing 146,000 through 1918.

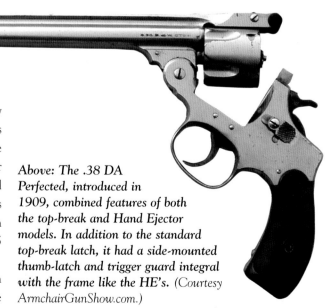

Above: The .38 DA Perfected, introduced in 1909, combined features of both the top-break and Hand Ejector models. In addition to the standard top-break latch, it had a side-mounted thumb-latch and trigger guard integral with the frame like the HE's. (Courtesy ArmchairGunShow.com.)

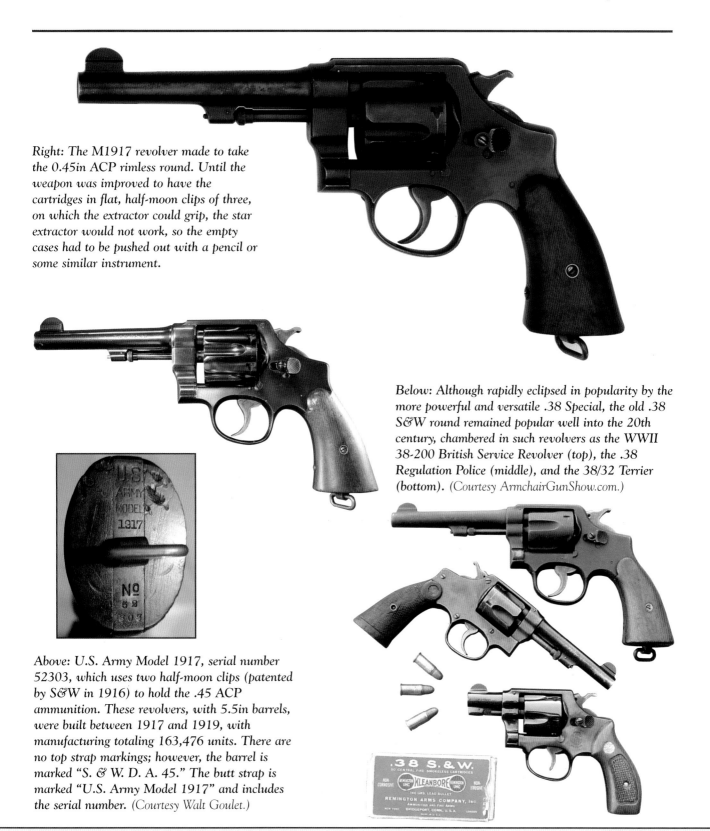

Right: The M1917 revolver made to take the 0.45in ACP rimless round. Until the weapon was improved to have the cartridges in flat, half-moon clips of three, on which the extractor could grip, the star extractor would not work, so the empty cases had to be pushed out with a pencil or some similar instrument.

Below: Although rapidly eclipsed in popularity by the more powerful and versatile .38 Special, the old .38 S&W round remained popular well into the 20th century, chambered in such revolvers as the WWII 38-200 British Service Revolver (top), the .38 Regulation Police (middle), and the 38/32 Terrier (bottom). (Courtesy ArmchairGunShow.com.)

Above: U.S. Army Model 1917, serial number 52303, which uses two half-moon clips (patented by S&W in 1916) to hold the .45 ACP ammunition. These revolvers, with 5.5in barrels, were built between 1917 and 1919, with manufacturing totaling 163,476 units. There are no top strap markings; however, the barrel is marked "S. & W. D. A. 45." The butt strap is marked "U.S. Army Model 1917" and includes the serial number. (Courtesy Walt Goulet.)

.32 AND .32-20 HAND EJECTOR MODELS TO 1942

Type: hand ejector swing-out cylinder, I and J frames.

Capacity: six-shot revolver.

Barrel lengths: 3¼ to 6½in.

Manufactured: 1896 to 1942.

Quantity: .32 (S&W Long cartridge), 393,939; .32-20 cartridge, 188,676.

Variations: .32, First and Third Models and five changes; earliest had cylinder latch combined with ejector rod; .32-20, called Second Model, four changes.

THE .357 AND .44 MAGNUMS, AND SEMI-AUTOS

After World War I, in common with the rest of the firearms industry, Smith & Wesson faced serious problems in reconverting to civilian production and maintaining a stable financial base. There was a large supply of .45in caliber U.S. Service model revolvers and parts that were difficult to convert to smaller revolvers that could be sold in the private market. Also, there was a flood of inferior,

lower-priced, foreign-made arms of similar appearance to Smith & Wesson's, and this caused serious competition. The end of the war produced an anti-gun movement which tried to stop the production of firearms and restrict firearms ownership. The company began to operate in the red.

The third generation of Wessons took over in 1920, at the death of the then president Joseph Wesson. Harold, son of Frank Luther Wesson, became the company's fourth president. The trust managing the company was dissolved, and by 1922 Harold was confirmed as the chief executive. An engineer by training from the Massachusetts Institute of Technology, he believed that the company had to diversify into new products. However, similarly to the experience of the Winchester Company, none of these other products produced any significant profit, except that the manufacture of handcuffs was begun and still continues today. Among the new products that were tried were washing machines and razor blade sharpeners, and there was a major venture into the design of toilet flush valves. While Smith & Wesson avoided Winchester's fate of being acquired by another company (Olin, in 1932), the company managed to hold on until 1939 when it was rescued by an influx of funds from the British military. A favorable result of the flush valve venture was that a Swedish engineer, Carl Hellstrom, was called in to improve the valve's

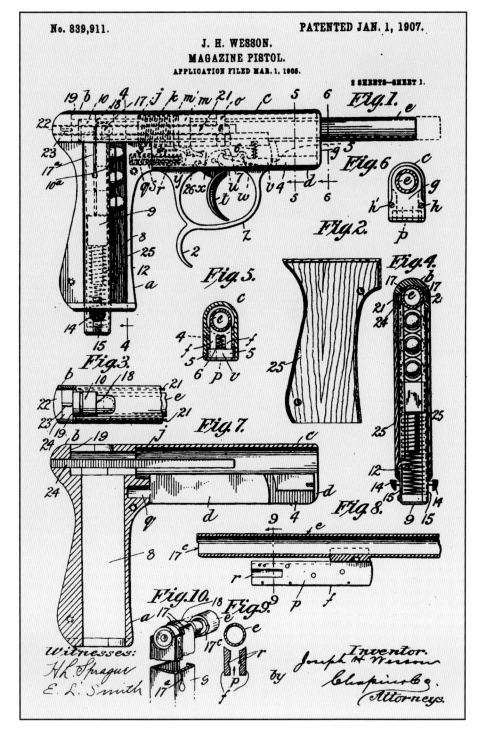

Left: Some of the drawings accompanying Joseph H. Wesson's Patent No. 839,911, dated January 1, 1907, in relation to a "magazine-pistol" of the sliding-barrel type.

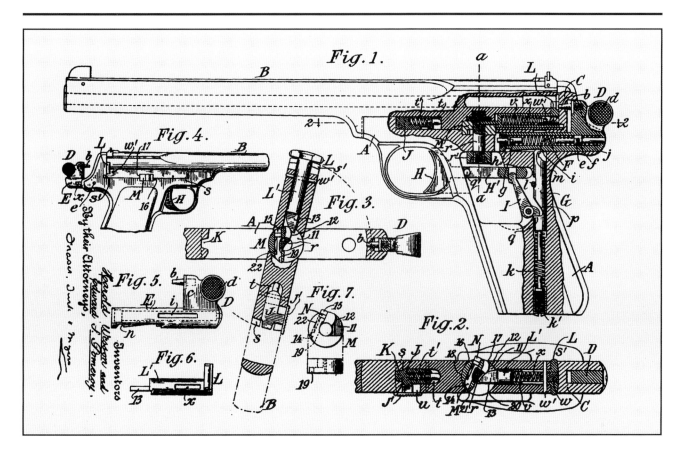

design, after which he became plant superintendent and a very effective president starting in 1946.

Before and after World War I, Smith & Wesson made its first efforts to market an automatic pistol (actually semiautomatic in that the trigger has to be pulled for each shot, but "automatic" is the usual terminology). In 1909 Joe Wesson, who was alternately sharing the presidency of the

Above: On December 4, 1923, Harold Wesson and Edward S. Pomeroy were granted Patent No. 1,476,125 in relation to, as their specification statement informs us, "pistols designed particularly for use in target practice, although applicable for other purposes. For such use it is desirable to have a long barrel and a comparatively heavy stock, so that the center of gravity shall be kept as low as possible, in order thereby to minimize the tendency of the recoil to throw up the muzzle when firing. The present invention attains these advantages and also shortens the pistol as much as possible without reducing the length of the barrel from its standard length (of ten inches)."

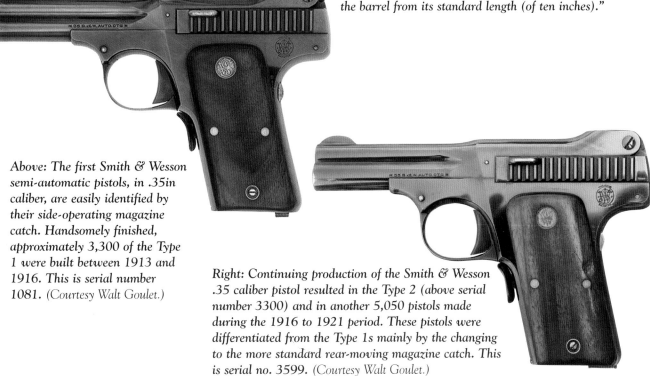

Above: The first Smith & Wesson semi-automatic pistols, in .35in caliber, are easily identified by their side-operating magazine catch. Handsomely finished, approximately 3,300 of the Type 1 were built between 1913 and 1916. This is serial number 1081. (Courtesy Walt Goulet.)

Right: Continuing production of the Smith & Wesson .35 caliber pistol resulted in the Type 2 (above serial number 3300) and in another 5,050 pistols made during the 1916 to 1921 period. These pistols were differentiated from the Type 1s mainly by the changing to the more standard rear-moving magazine catch. This is serial no. 3599. (Courtesy Walt Goulet.)

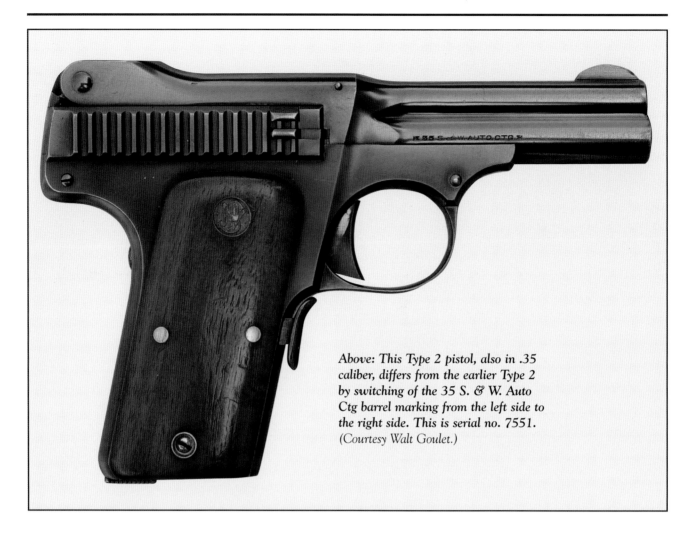

Above: This Type 2 pistol, also in .35 caliber, differs from the earlier Type 2 by switching of the 35 S. & W. Auto Ctg barrel marking from the left side to the right side. This is serial no. 7551. (Courtesy Walt Goulet.)

company with Harold Wesson, met a Belgian inventor, Charles Philibert Clement, and then purchased his 1910 patent for a small automatic pistol with the barrel below the recoil spring, reducing the recoil since the barrel was closer to the shooter's hand. Joe developed the design further, together with a .35in cartridge, helped by the Remington Arms Company. The pistol also included a grip safety on the front side of the grip, as compared with the Colt Model 1903 in .32in and .380 calibers. The pistol sold well, but production was stopped after only six months because of war production of revolvers for the British. In 1921 the company started to redesign this automatic to use the .32 ACP

Above: Smith & Wesson manufactured its .32 caliber semi-automatic in 1924 with sales proceeding until 1927. The company made only 957 of these high-quality, attractive and fine, but expensive .32 caliber pistols, of which this is serial no. 250. (Courtesy Walt Goulet.)

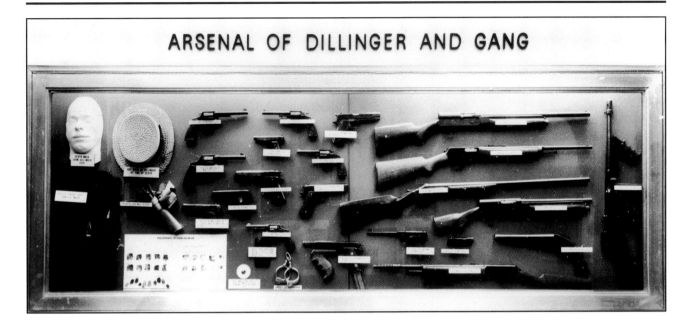

ARSENAL OF DILLINGER AND GANG

cartridge and sales began in 1924 with a more streamlined design, but it was more expensive than the competing Colt. Sales were slow, being discontinued in 1937.

The Great Depression starting in 1929 affected Smith & Wesson as well as all the other firearms manufacturers, but the gloomy state of Smith & Wesson's production was dramatically changed, at least as the foundation for future growth, by a startling invention introduced in 1935, the .357 Magnum. This was in response to the crime wave in the 1920s related to the Volstead Act which made liquor illegal in the United States, otherwise known as Prohibition (1920-1933). This was an era of violent struggles between organized crime syndicates or gangs for control of illegal manufacture and distribution of liquor. Gang murders were rife, and police departments and Federal officers, with their

Above: This is part of the arsenal of hoodlum John Dillinger and his gang (and including the rather gruesome death mask of Dillinger). During the days of Prohibition, America's law enforcement officers were often out-gunned by the criminals they tried to control, as witnessed by this collection of submachine guns, shotguns, rifles and pistols and revolvers, including Smith & Wesson arms. (Courtesy FBI.)

.38 caliber revolvers, were often outgunned by these lawless elements. Many of the .45 caliber military automatics found their way into private hands, and the gangsters were even using the Thompson submachine guns (popularly known as the "Tommygun" or " Chicago Piano") which Colt's began to manufacture in 1920. Smith & Wesson first tried to introduce a more powerful cartridge in 1930 with the .38/44

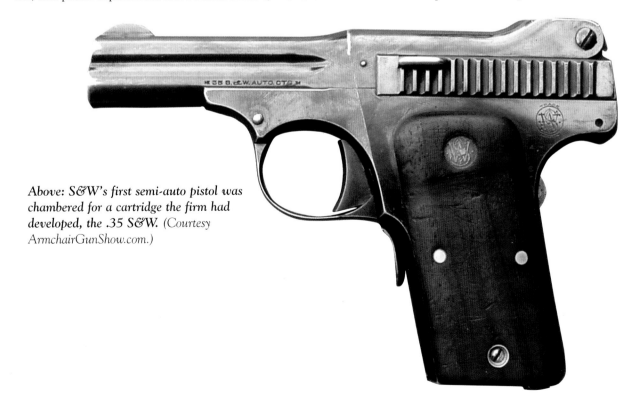

Above: S&W's first semi-auto pistol was chambered for a cartridge the firm had developed, the .35 S&W. (Courtesy ArmchairGunShow.com.)

Heavy Duty revolver using the large N frame and a special high-velocity .38 Special cartridge. The gun was popular with law enforcement agencies and over 11,000 were sold up to 1941. There was also an unsuccessful attempt made to market this revolver in .45in caliber.

Smith & Wesson's next attempt to meet this challenge was in 1935, and this time it succeeded far beyond its expectations. The new gun and cartridge were the .357in Magnum, and it was revolutionary in terms of the use of the handgun in both law enforcement and in private hands, and even for hunting big game. Roy Jinks enthuses: "The words .357 *Magnum* elicit a very reverent feeling on the part of handgun users, for it was with this Smith & Wesson model that the world was launched into a *Magnum* age."

Supica and Nahas go even further in their praise: "The development of the .357 Magnum in 1935 may be viewed as the birth of the modern handgun era. It introduced a power level in handguns unknown before that time. According to the latest statistics on police shootings, the .357 Magnum remains unmatched, even today, as an effective defensive round. The beginnings of handgun hunting as something more serious than a stunt can be traced to the power and relatively flat trajectory of the .357 Magnum."

The idea for the new handgun began in the 1920s when arms and ammunition writer Philip Sharpe urged the company to develop a more powerful cartridge than the .38 Special. Douglas Wesson, the son of Joe Wesson, was brought into the picture. He had served in World War I, becoming a colonel of Reserves, and had worked for the Winchester company, which made cartridges as well as rifles. Smith & Wesson's new cartridge, using a case 1/8in longer than the .38 Special, according to writer Dick Metcalf, was substantially more powerful than any previous any type had ever offered (today it is toned down somewhat to meet international specifications). It produced the desired effect for use by the police: it would penetrate three thicknesses of contemporary "bullet-proof" vests, managed to penetrate duralumin plates and, fired through the hood of a car idling at high speed, would both stop and disable its engine. Legend has it that Colonel Wesson, a *bon vivant* of champagne, gave it the name Magnum because of his fondness for the oversized bottle.

The new revolver issued in 1935 for this cartridge was designed on Smith & Wesson's large N frame, and was offered as a luxury custom model with a target configuration and a range of options for barrel lengths, sights, and grips. The price, $60, was higher than any other company handgun. Each purchaser was given a numbered registration certificate.

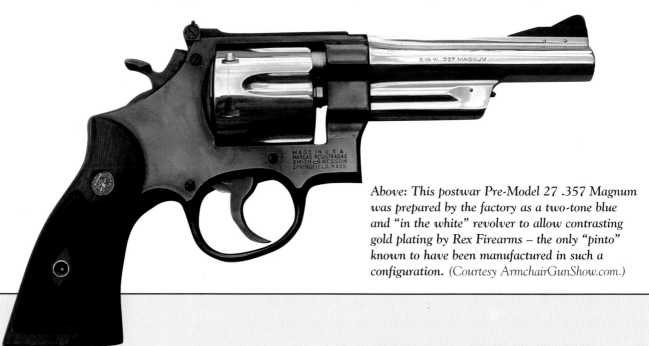

Above: This postwar Pre-Model 27 .357 Magnum was prepared by the factory as a two-tone blue and "in the white" revolver to allow contrasting gold plating by Rex Firearms – the only "pinto" known to have been manufactured in such a configuration. (Courtesy ArmchairGunShow.com.)

.357 MAGNUM HAND EJECTOR, AND LATER MODELS 27 AND 28

Type: Swing-out cylinder revolver, K and N frame.

Capacity: six shots.

Barrel lengths: 3½ to 8¾in, pinned barrel and extractor shroud.

Made: Hand Ejector 1935 to 1939: Model 27, The .357 Magnum, 1948 to 1994; Model 28, The Highway Patrolman, 1954 to 1986.

Quantity: Hand Ejector, about 5,224; Models 27 and 28, not published.

Variations: Model 27 with new hammer block and postwar improvements, S serial number prefix; Model 28, utility version, N serial number prefix; smaller K frame introduced in 1955 as the Combat Magnum.

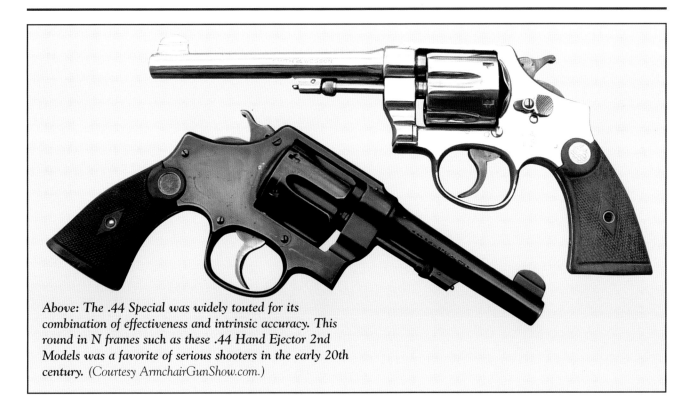

Above: The .44 Special was widely touted for its combination of effectiveness and intrinsic accuracy. This round in N frames such as these .44 Hand Ejector 2nd Models was a favorite of serious shooters in the early 20th century. (Courtesy ArmchairGunShow.com.)

The company was simply overwhelmed with orders for the firearm. After 1938, the registration certificates were dropped at serial number 5,500. Up to 1941, when production was stopped to make way for war models, some 6,642 had been made. It was reintroduced in 1948 as the Model 27, and continued in production until 1994. Today the cartridge is still used, now with medium instead of large frame models.

The first revolver produced in 1935 was presented to J. Edgar Hoover, and its use by the FBI was legendary. One story concerned agent Walter Walsh who was sent to Bangor, Maine, in 1937 to investigate some gangsters who were trying to order some machine guns. He set up an ambush for the Al Brady gang at a local gunshop, and in a gun battle on the sidewalk, where Walsh was wounded, he dropped a gangster who turned out to be Al Brady himself (two more gangsters were shut inside the store). Other lawmen noted for their speed on the draw with the .357 Magnum were Oklahoman Gelly Brice, veteran of a number of shootouts, Border Patrolman Bill Jordan, and Texas Ranger Arthur Hill. General George Patton ordered this model with a 3½in barrel and ivory grips, carrying it and a Colt Peacemaker in a pair of holsters seen in photographs of him throughout World War II.

The .357 Magnum also ushered in the era of big game hunting with a handgun. Col. Wesson made a hunting trip west to Wyoming, following the footsteps of Grand Duke Alexis, whose successful use of the Model 3 sparked the large orders by the Russian military in the 1870s. Wesson brought back reports of taking antelope, elk, and moose. However, it was not until the later introduction of the .44 Magnum that handguns were used extensively for hunting.

Military models

Smith & Wesson military models were somewhat in evidence between World Wars I and II, particularly the .45 ACP Second Model Hand Ejector of 1915, with many being sold as surplus on the civilian market. The Peters Cartridge Company produced a special rimmed .45in caliber round which avoided the use of the half moon clip, and Smith &

Above: Everything about this member of the U.S. Coast Guard Beach Patrol – from the uniform to the S&W .38 revolver – looks new and unused in the early days of World War II. The official caption says: "Coast Guardsmen maintain constant vigil on ocean outposts, ready to halt enemy espionage agents and saboteurs before they land." (Courtesy National Archives.)

Left: Firearms training, using Smith & Wesson revolvers, at the "Service School for Negro shore patrolmen," Great Lakes Naval Training Station, Illinois, November 1943. (Courtesy National Archives.)

Wesson itself offered replacement cylinders so that civilian owners could convert the guns to fire standard .45 Colt ammunition.

Writer Garry James notes that many of the Smith & Wesson 1917s which had been retained by the U.S. Army were issued as "retreads" in World War II to second line troops, although some officers preferred them over their Colt automatics. Also, in 1932 the Marines ordered 21,000 Military and Police model revolvers in .38in caliber, and just before World War II some 3,000 Smith & Wesson handguns were issued to the U.S. Naval Civilian Police Corps. Guns with these markings command a premium on the collectors' market.

As war clouds thickened in Europe and the German Army marched into Poland on September 1, 1939, setting off World War II, the British again approached Smith & Wesson as they had done in World War I. This time they invited the company to produce a light automatic-firing assault rifle. The company promptly obliged with the Model 1940 Light Rifle in 9mm caliber, with a large magazine below the forestock. Unfortunately, the cartridge it was designed for was lighter than the 9mm predominantly used by the British, and after a series of misfires because of the different cartridges, the British scrapped the shipments that started to be made and cancelled the order, leaving Smith & Wesson with the obligation of repaying the amount of $1,000,000 which had been advanced.

However, under the leadership of plant superintendent C. R. Hellstrom, an agreement was soon reached under which the order would be filled by revolvers instead of rifles. The company's entire production facilities were turned over to this revolver, which was designed for the .38 Smith &

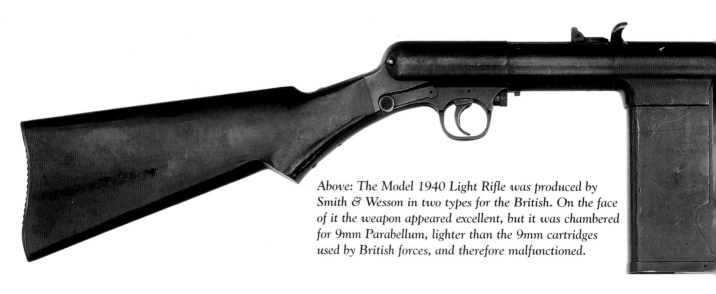

Above: The Model 1940 Light Rifle was produced by Smith & Wesson in two types for the British. On the face of it the weapon appeared excellent, but it was chambered for 9mm Parabellum, lighter than the 9mm cartridges used by British forces, and therefore malfunctioned.

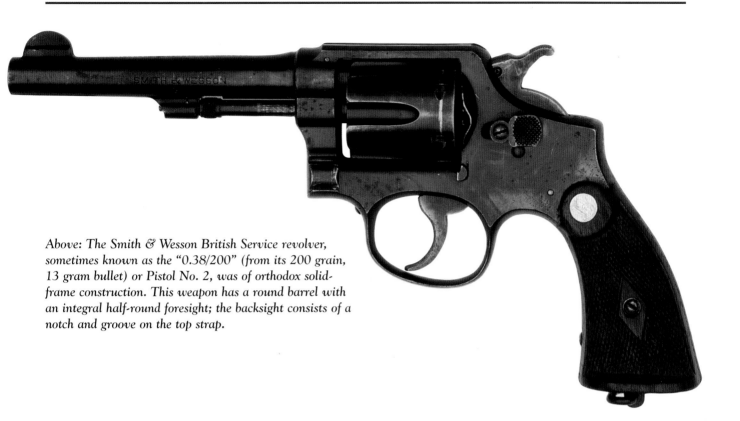

Above: The Smith & Wesson British Service revolver, sometimes known as the "0.38/200" (from its 200 grain, 13 gram bullet) or Pistol No. 2, was of orthodox solid-frame construction. This weapon has a round barrel with an integral half-round foresight; the backsight consists of a notch and groove on the top strap.

Wesson cartridge instead of the .38 Special to meet the British requirements. After that, the production of .38 Special revolvers was resumed, and then accelerated for American service requirements.

During the war a total of 568,204 revolvers were produced for the British and the other Commonwealth nations, and a further 242,915 for the American armed forces. Both models are famous for the prefix V given the serial numbers starting on April 24, 1942, when those of the original Model 1905 reached 1,000,000. The revolvers were promptly dubbed Victory Models and have been known as such ever since.

Right: Private Harry Jacobs of HDQ Troop, 1st Cavalry, finalises preparation of his S&W Military & Police Model during the island-hopping campaign, October 2, 1944. (Courtesy National Archives.)

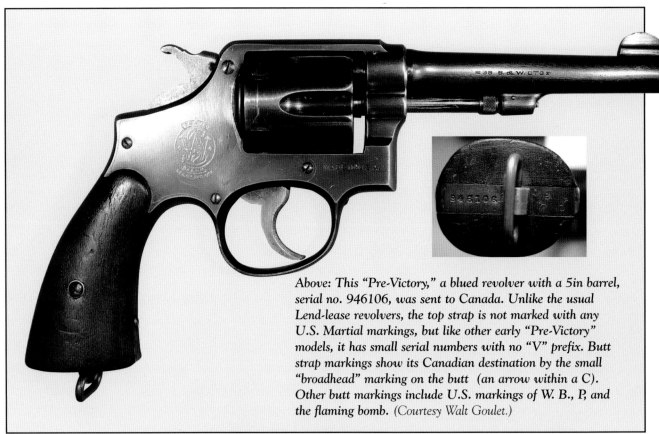

Above: This "Pre-Victory," a blued revolver with a 5in barrel, serial no. 946106, was sent to Canada. Unlike the usual Lend-lease revolvers, the top strap is not marked with any U.S. Martial markings, but like other early "Pre-Victory" models, it has small serial numbers with no "V" prefix. Butt strap markings show its Canadian destination by the small "broadhead" marking on the butt (an arrow within a C). Other butt markings include U.S. markings of W. B., P, and the flaming bomb. *(Courtesy Walt Goulet.)*

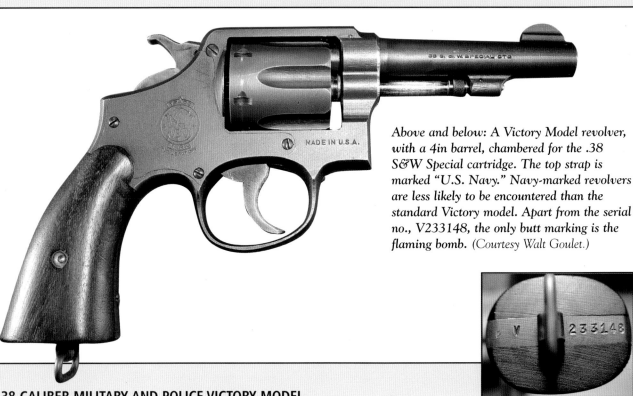

Above and below: A Victory Model revolver, with a 4in barrel, chambered for the .38 S&W Special cartridge. The top strap is marked "U.S. Navy." Navy-marked revolvers are less likely to be encountered than the standard Victory model. Apart from the serial no., V233148, the only butt marking is the flaming bomb. *(Courtesy Walt Goulet.)*

.38 CALIBER MILITARY AND POLICE VICTORY MODEL

Type: swing-out cylinder revolver, K frame.

Capacity: six shots.

Barrel lengths: British service, 4, 5, and 6in; American service, 2 and 4in.

Manufactured: 1939-1945.

Quantity: British service 568,204; American service, over 242,915.

Variations: British service, blued up to April 19, 1942, after that all production Parkerized (dull) finish; after December 1944, added hammer block due to a report of an American sailor killed from a dropped revolver.

Aircrew firearms

Although the Colt Model 1911 .45 caliber automatic was the standard sidearm of World War I and was also made by other contractors, the Smith & Wesson Victory Models were important for support troops, the OSS (Office of Strategic Services), and on the home front. Writer Garry James notes that its most glamorous use was as an airman's sidearm. He has an example with a naval pilot's name and squadron scratched on the butt. The unit apparently flew F6F Hellcats, and destroyed 57 enemy aircraft in one day at Iwo Jima.

Following World War II, Smith & Wesson's only substantial military contract was in the 1950s for an aluminum frame revolver called the USAF-M13 "Aircrewman." The intention was to reduce the weight of the sidearms carried by aircrew when ejecting from aircraft. Winning a competition with Colt, the company designed a swing-out cylinder revolver with a K frame, using the .38 Special cartridge. Some 40,000 were made, in several variations. However, at that point, the Air Force decided that the revolvers were not strong enough to stand up under

Below: Comdr. David Campbell, USN (right), has his Victory Model revolver in the standard Navy pattern shoulder holster. He and his officer colleague, Lt. Comdr. James Rigg, proudly display the VF-15 success rate aboard the carrier USS Essex, *August 8, 1944. (Courtesy National Archives.)*

Above: During the early 1960s, the U.S. government supplied S&W .38in caliber revolvers for a training scheme designed to give military defense instruction to more than a million South Vietnamese boys and girls of the "Republic Youth Movement" in support of Ngo Dinh Diem's ruling party. (Courtesy National Archives.)

Above: During the Vietnam War the U.S. Navy SEALs special-ordered suppressed, black-finished, stainless steel versions of the Model 39 DA 9mm pistol, nicknamed "Hushpuppy" but officially designated Mk22 Model O. At top is a single-stack version, while below it is the 14-round double-stack version which later was developed into the commercial Model 59. (Courtesy Smith & Wesson.)

repeated firing, and the order was cancelled and most of the guns destroyed. The few that were sold as surplus in the 1960s are prized by collectors; they are stamped "Property Of U.S. Air Force, and "Revolver, Light-Weight, M13."

There were three other unusual ventures into military firearms by Smith & Wesson. In 1968 the company produced its first fully automatic firearm, the Model 76. It was of simple, inexpensive construction like the World War II British Sten or the American "Grease Gun," with seamless tubing, a folding stock, and a simple welded sight. Production was stopped because of lack of sales. A second item, ordered by the U.S. Navy SEALs in 1968, was a silenced version of a modified 9mm semi-automatic pistol developed by the company for civilian use, made available for use in Vietnam. Finally, the military adapted the .44 Magnum introduced by Smith & Wesson in 1955 for use as a "Tunnel Gun," with a smoothbore barrel and a steel cartridge with a piston which propelled a sabot shot and small lead balls noiselessly, clearing the kind of tunnel used

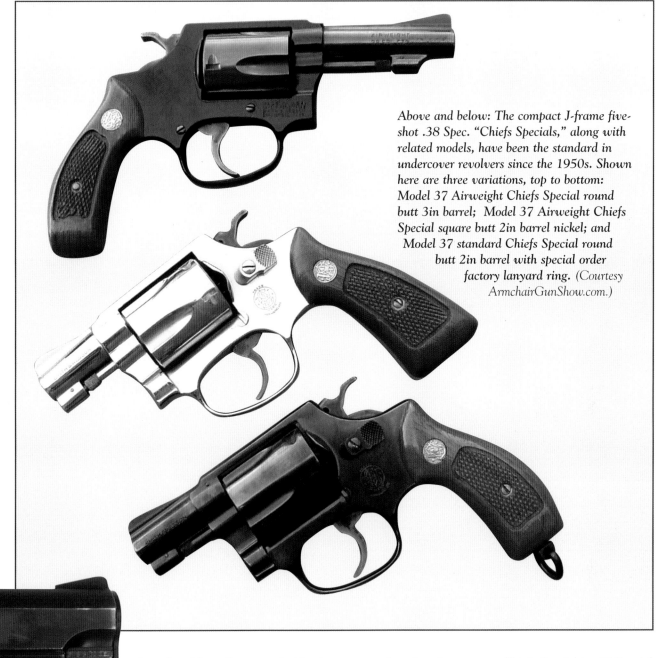

Above and below: The compact J-frame five-shot .38 Spec. "Chiefs Specials," along with related models, have been the standard in undercover revolvers since the 1950s. Shown here are three variations, top to bottom: Model 37 Airweight Chiefs Special round butt 3in barrel; Model 37 Airweight Chiefs Special square butt 2in barrel nickel; and Model 37 standard Chiefs Special round butt 2in barrel with special order factory lanyard ring. (Courtesy ArmchairGunShow.com.)

by the Viet Cong and North Vietnamese. It was officially termed the QSPR (Quiet Special Purpose Revolver), but there is no published record of its actual use.

A Smith & Wesson innovation on the civilian market was actually put to extensive use in Vietnam, according to Timothy Mullin in *Greatest Combat Pistols*. This was the introduction of the first stainless steel revolver, the Model 60. Before 1965 all revolvers were made of carbon steel or, in lightweight models, aluminum alloy, with the finish the traditional blued or nickel plated. Now, most handguns are made in stainless steel, finished bright, because of its reduced maintenance and increased finish durability. The Model 60

Left: The 9mm Model 39 pistol worked on double action for the first shot, followed by single action for all subsequent shots. There was a square ramp foresight, and a square notch backsight, click-adjustable for windage only.

was produced as the compact Chiefs Special in .38 Special caliber, and was greatly in demand, as Mullin puts it, by everybody who knew anything about handguns and was anticipating going to Vietnam. He "remembers the factory-list price of an M60 being $85 and people happily buying them for $200. Leroy Thompson reports that among his operational group in Vietnam, an M60 could be swapped for anything you really wanted: booze, guns, or women, he sold his M60 for $500 on the way back home in 1968." It was an ideal weapon for the company-grade infantry officer in Vietnam; he carried it in his breast pocket, it being light and compact and especially not subject to rusting in the humid jungle.

Mullin notes that Smith & Wesson's Model 39 Double Action automatic was also carried by many soldiers in Vietnam, and the Air Force purchased a small quantity. Thus, between revolvers and automatics, Smith & Wesson had an extensive war record in Vietnam, even though this was mainly through the civilian market.

Left: Loading a S&W .22in Model 41 Autoloading target pistol, a specialist weapon for target-shooting (note adjustable sights) introduced in 1957.

Hellstrom's legacy

The end of World War II did not cause major problems for Smith & Wesson, unlike its experience after World War I. C. R. Hellstrom, who had been the plant superintendent as related above, was made president of the company in 1946. He was paid a fixed salary plus a percentage of the company's profits, which helped to make him one of the highest paid executives in the United States. The family's faith in him was evidently justified: he set a policy of concentrating on the company's strength, the manufacture of handguns (with the only exception that the manufacture of handcuffs was resumed in 1952). During the war he had established a branch factory for drop forging on Roosevelt Boulevard on the outskirts of Springfield; Hellstrom moved the entire operation to the site, opening a new plant covering an area of 270,000 square feet in 1950. This was considered the most modern revolver plant in the world.

But Carl Hellstrom died suddenly of a heart attack in 1963, and was mourned by all the company employees, who he had considered to be his family. After that, the company's prosperity attracted a successful tender offer by a major conglomerate, Bangor Punta. Cynthia Wesson, grand-daughter of D. B. Wesson, gave the proceeds of the sale of her stock to the company employees. William Gunn, who had been plant superintendent under Hellstrom, became president under Bangor Punta and added the line of new products and special facilities such as the Police Academy which continue today and are described in the next chapter. In 1984 another conglomerate, Lear Siegler, bought Bangor Punta, with Smith & Wesson as part of the package, and the company in turn was purchased by Forstmann Little and Company in 1986, then by Tomkins plc of England in 1987, and finally by its present owner, Saf-T-Hammer, under Robert L. Scott, a former Smith & Wesson vice-president, in 2001.

It is not the intention of this book to detail all of the many models and variations of Smith & Wesson revolvers, particularly as they proliferated after World War II. One observer commented that the company's production was like the "Gun of the Week," and a major strength of the company has been its ability to meet many different markets for handguns, not only in the United States, but worldwide, both military and civilian. We will concentrate here on the two blockbuster models which the company pioneered and on which most of its present-day success is based, the .44 Magnum and the 9mm semi-automatic. (The reader is referred particularly to the Supica and Nahas *Standard Catalog of Smith & Wesson*, Second Edition 2002, for a listing and description of all the various models, complete even to an estimate of their collector's value.)

"Make my day"

Few moviegoers with any interest in firearms are unfamiliar with the massive revolver carried by Clint Eastwood as police detective "Dirty Harry," and his warning to the criminal that it was "the most powerful handgun in the world" and would "blow his head clean off." In a sequel, he again aimed the revolver and dared the perpetrator of the crime to "Make my day" (the criminal did not; he surrendered). The revolver, in effect Eastwood's co-star, was the Smith & Wesson .44 Magnum.

The revolver was actually launched as the Model 29 well before Eastwood's movie was released in 1972. It was designed as an expensive custom model, and attracted interest mainly among sportsmen interested in hunting with handguns. Unexpectedly, its popularity exploded with the "Dirty Harry" movie and Smith & Wesson was flooded with orders. The craze lasted about five years, but the company's 2002 catalog listed four models in .44 Magnum, plus one in .44 S&W Special; the .44 Magnums were shown as also taking the .44 S&W Special cartridge, which has somewhat lower power and therefore lower recoil.

It is reported that many purchasers are attracted by the Model 29's glamor and massive appearance, but are so intimidated by its loud report and heavy recoil that they hardly if ever fire the gun! A modification offered by the company to lessen the "kick" is "porting": putting a slot on top of the barrel close to the muzzle, slanted away from the shooter, to allow some gas to escape before reaching the muzzle. This increases the noise of the gun firing to some extent.

Above: Clint Eastwood made movie-goers' day when, as truculent San Francisco cop "Dirty Harry" Callahan, he informs a criminal that the Smith & Wesson Model 29 .44 Magnum could blow his head off. The combination of Eastwood and firearm was certainly explosive, propelling a career on the one hand and sales on the other. (Courtesy Photofest, NYC, NY.)

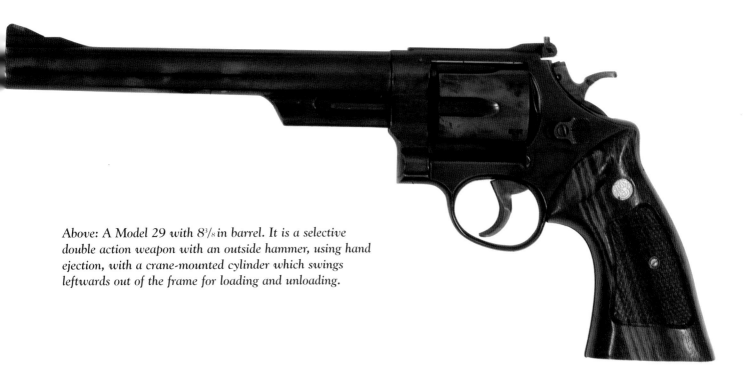

Above: A Model 29 with 8³/₈ in barrel. It is a selective double action weapon with an outside hammer, using hand ejection, with a crane-mounted cylinder which swings leftwards out of the frame for loading and unloading.

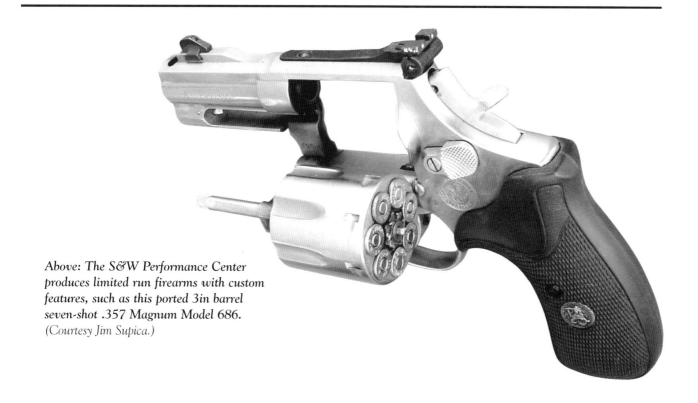

Above: The S&W Performance Center produces limited run firearms with custom features, such as this ported 3in barrel seven-shot .357 Magnum Model 686. (Courtesy Jim Supica.)

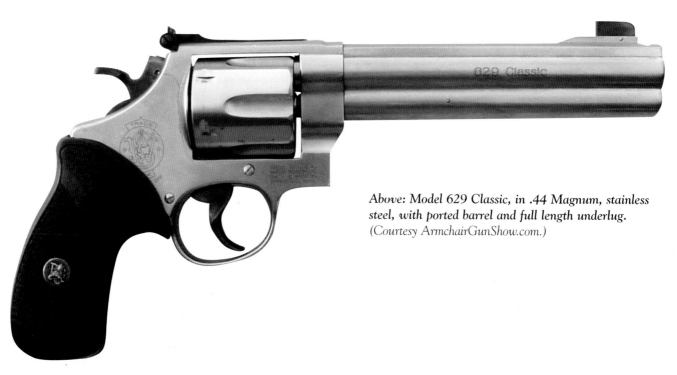

Above: Model 629 Classic, in .44 Magnum, stainless steel, with ported barrel and full length underlug. (Courtesy ArmchairGunShow.com.)

MODEL 29 .44 MAGNUM

Type: swing-out cylinder revolver on square-butt N target frame.

Capacity: six shots.

Barrel lengths: 4 to 8³/₈in.

Manufactured: 1955 to 1999; later versions made to the present.

Quantity: from serial numbers, apparently over 800,000.

Variations: N serial number prefix changed to S in 1969; cylinder counterbore and pinned barrel eliminated in 1982; special issues, the Silhouette, the .44 Classic, the .44 Classic DX, the .44 Magna Classic.

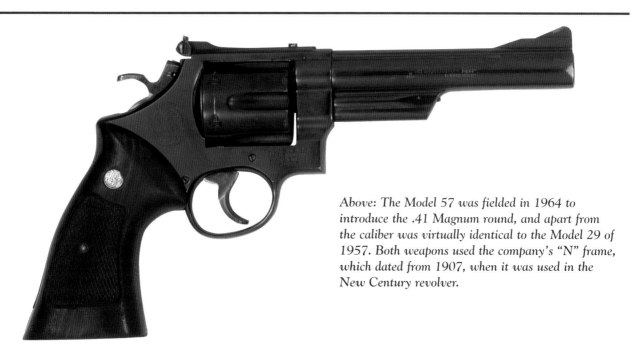

Above: The Model 57 was fielded in 1964 to introduce the .41 Magnum round, and apart from the caliber was virtually identical to the Model 29 of 1957. Both weapons used the company's "N" frame, which dated from 1907, when it was used in the New Century revolver.

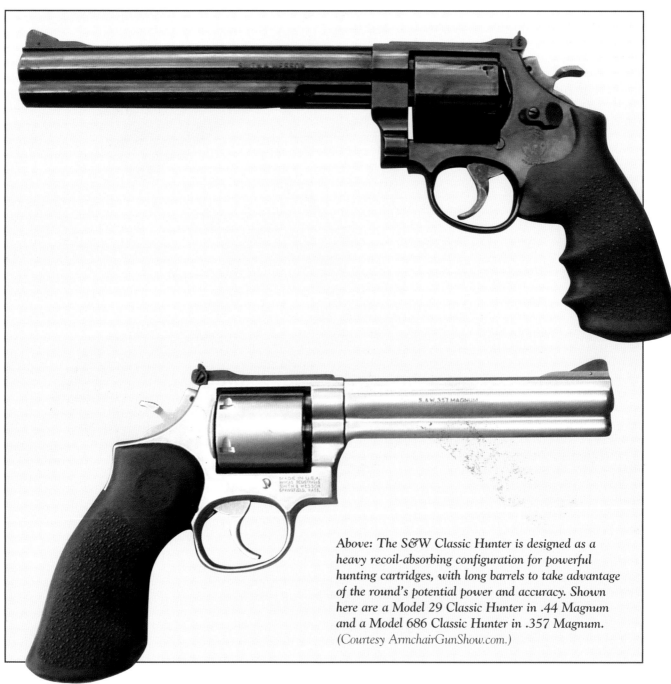

Above: The S&W Classic Hunter is designed as a heavy recoil-absorbing configuration for powerful hunting cartridges, with long barrels to take advantage of the round's potential power and accuracy. Shown here are a Model 29 Classic Hunter in .44 Magnum and a Model 686 Classic Hunter in .357 Magnum. (Courtesy ArmchairGunShow.com.)

The .44 Magnum owes its origin to Elmer Keith, a longtime firearms expert and writer known as the "Idaho Cowboy," who consulted with Douglas Wesson when the .357 Magnum was introduced in 1935, and who experimented with larger cartridges for long-range target and big game hunting use. He visited with C. R. Hellstrom of Smith & Wesson and C. G. Peterson of Remington while on a trip east in 1953, and finally convinced the two of the feasibility of an oversized cartridge in .44in caliber. Once the pistol began to be produced, Keith helped make long-range pistol target shooting a popular sport. In the fall of 1956, in a demonstration of the .44 Magnum revolver's effectiveness in hunting big game, he brought down a mule deer buck that had been wounded by a .300 Winchester rifle; the distance was between 500 and 600 yards. There was some controversy, and there may still be, over handgun hunting, and it is a sport considered appropriate only for experts. Its appeal was summed up by a statement from Smith & Wesson

Above: Introduced in 1954, the S&W Model 39 (bottom) was the first American-made double action semi-auto pistol. In 1971, S&W increased the magazine capacity using a double stack column, and introduced the Model 59 (top) as the first of the high-capacity double action 9mm semi-auto pistols which gained rapid popularity for police use and came to be known generically by the nickname "Wonder-Nines." (Courtesy ArmchairGunShow.com.)

Above: Model 422 semi-auto in .22 L.R., with non-factory scope and mount. (Courtesy Jim Supica.)

Above: S&W Model 3914, serial no. TDF-0001, first production run. It is a Third Generation 9mm auto-pistol in popular slim profile compact version, well suited for concealed carry. (Courtesy Jim Supica.)

MODEL 39 9MM SEMI-AUTOMATIC AND DOUBLE ACTION, HAMMER DROP SAFETY

Capacity: eight-round magazine.

Barrel length: 4in.

Manufactured: 1954 to 1971; Second Generation (Model 59) 1971 to 1988; Third Generation (1000 series, 10mm), 1984 to 1999. Later versions made to the present.

Quantity: not published.

Variations: First Generation, double column magazine with 15 rounds introduced after 1959; Second Generation, improvements made in feeding and to reduce jamming; Third Generation, updated manufacturing process, improved sights, and wrap-around grip.

Above: S&W's Model 4500 series pistols fire the .45in ACP round. The three firearms in the series are Models 4506, 4566 and 4586, and are known as the "Third Generation." The firearm shown is a 4506, with 5in barrel.

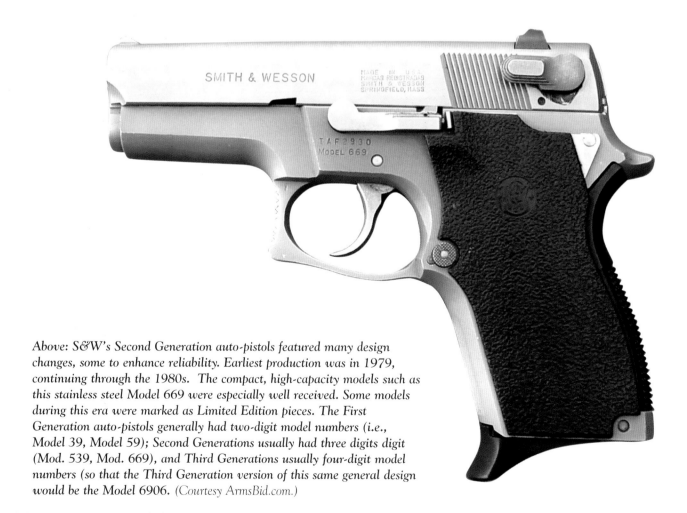

Above: S&W's Second Generation auto-pistols featured many design changes, some to enhance reliability. Earliest production was in 1979, continuing through the 1980s. The compact, high-capacity models such as this stainless steel Wessson 669 were especially well received. Some models during this era were marked as Limited Edition pieces. The First Generation auto-pistols generally had two-digit model numbers (i.e., Model 39, Model 59); Second Generations usually had three digits digit (Mod. 539, Mod. 669), and Third Generations usually four-digit model numbers (so that the Third Generation version of this same general design would be the Model 6906. (Courtesy ArmsBid.com.)

Above: The Model 469 appeared in the 1970s to meet requests for a smaller ("chopped") automatic pistol and was based on the 14-shot Model 459. Its barrel was a half-inch shorter than that of the 459.

in the 1938 edition of *Burning Powder* as follows: "The ultimate in accomplishment, in skillful stalking, in accurate shooting, is realized when one captures his trophy with a handgun, and we can, without reservations recommend the Magnum for big-game hunting . . . we believe this kind of hunting requires more skill in stalking and more skill in shooting, and is therefore more thrilling and more satisfactory than with a rifle."

Model 39 semi-auto

The second epoch-making advance in handguns pioneered by Smith & Wesson in the postwar period was its Model 39 semi-automatic in .99mm caliber. Now developed mainly into the .40 caliber S&W instead of 9mm for more power, the Smith & Wesson versions of this handgun are not as well known as the .44 Magnum, but the numbers involved may be larger. For example, a recent survey by Wiley Clapp reported in *American Rifleman* noted that one-fourth of all the state police departments in the United States were using

S&W automatics (and 27 were using the .40 S&W cartridge).

Smith & Wesson's Model 39, introduced in 1955, was the first American-made large caliber semi-automatic pistol. The American military had been impressed with the German P-38, which had replaced the Luger during World War II as the major German Army sidearm, and approached Smith & Wesson about designing a similar pistol. The traditional Colt U.S. Model 1911 automatic was a very effective military handgun, but had a serious disadvantage: it could not be carried in a ready-to-fire position. The safest way to carry it is without a cartridge in the chamber, meaning that the user has to pull back the slide to cock the hammer before firing. A cartridge can be placed in the chamber and the hammer cocked with the manual safety lever on; this requires only releasing the safety catch before firing. However, it was considered unsafe to carry the gun in this manner, with the hammer cocked, in case it would be dropped and the safety would come off or not operate.

The P-38 introduced a new mechanism, now in common use for most present day automatics, in which the first shot

Above: The result of a collaboration between Smith & Wesson and European Carl Walther, the Model SW99 is an advanced automatic pistol available in 9mm (with 4in barrel) or .40 S&W (with 4¹/₈in barrel). (Courtesy Smith & Wesson.)

is double action, that is, the movement of the trigger cocks the hammer. Before firing, the pistol is carried with the hammer down instead of cocked, and in fact even after it is cocked, such as happens after firing the first shot, a decocker lever can lower the hammer without its setting off the cartridge. The P-38 has the additional feature of a pin protruding from the rear of the slide when there is a cartridge in the chamber, so that the user can tell by feel if the gun is loaded. Also, the P-38 uses the 9mm Luger cartridge, which has more penetrating power than the .45 ACP cartridge used by the Colt Model 1911, and has a thinner shape, allowing more cartridges to be loaded into the magazine. Some modern automatics, like a later version of the Smith & Wesson 39, use a double stack magazine in the pistol's handle, thus nearly doubling the gun's capacity.

After further consideration and objections by aficionados of the Colt Model 1911, the Army decided not to adopt the new system. Accordingly, Smith & Wesson was left to recoup its development costs by sales on the private market, which at first were slow. However, there was a wave of civil unrest during the 1960s with the start of the Vietnam War, stimulating a move for greater firearm power for the police. The Illinois State Police decided to adopt the Smith & Wesson 39 in 1967, starting a movement by other police departments. When stories began to circulate about malfunctions and breakages with the new automatic, Smith & Wesson made improvements, and in 1980 came out with

a new line of automatics referred to as the Second Generation. Both double column pistols with a 20-round capacity and compact models with the original 14-round capacity were added to the standard new Model 439.

Spurred by a move by NATO to adopt a 9mm automatic, and to replace the long-service Colt M1911, the U.S. Army held a competition in 1984 for a new military sidearm. Smith & Wesson lost out to the Beretta, but had a failure rate in the tests of only 0.04 percent and an average of 2,500 rounds fired without a failure, which was an enviable record. At this point, influenced by the publicity about the Army trials, there was a stampede among U.S. police departments to adopt automatics instead of the traditional revolvers, and by manufacturers to design them (the "Wondernine Wars").

Smith & Wesson, in the thick of the competition, kept on making improvements to its automatic, as well as upgrading and modernizing its manufacturing processes, and introduced the Third Generation of the Model 39 in 1980. This featured improved sights with a lower profile and rounded edges to prevent snagging, and also white inserts with one dot on the front side and two on the rear, to help with shooting at dark targets or with low light. Wrap around grips were also added.

Another element in the competition was added in the non-military market in the mid-1980s when Gaston Glock's Austrian company introduced an automatic with a polymer frame (still with a steel barrel, contrary to rumors that it could not be detected at airports) and a new operating system in which firing did not completely retract the slide, substantially reducing the pressure the shooter has to exert on the trigger for double action. The pistol did not have an exposed hammer, being operated in double action only. There was no exterior safety, meaning that the pistol could be fired immediately without having to release a safety lever as was the case with the P-38 and the Smith & Wesson Model 39.

A design with no safety has the disadvantage of making the weapon easier for an assailant to use if he takes a police officer's gun away from him. The original version with the safety is still preferred by many departments, and is still offered by Smith & Wesson. The use of automatics is now universal among U.S. police departments, and Smith & Wesson has competitors other than Glock, such as SIG Arms, Beretta, and Ruger, as well Heckler and Koch which offers a pistol that can be converted either way (with or without the safety).

Smith & Wesson responded to Glock's competition in 1994 with its Sigma series of polymer frame automatics starting with the Model SW9F. In 2002 the company was offering six variations. There is no external manual safety and a round in the chamber can be fired with the magazine out of the pistol. The trigger pull is relatively stiff, providing

safety against accidental discharge (this system has supporters and detractors). An additional polymer frame automatic is offered with conventional safety features, co-designed and produced with Walther of Germany, called the Model SW99. Both have capacities of up to 16 rounds. At present, there is still another system on the market, by a competitor, Para-Ordnance, with "Light Double Action," in which the trigger pull is constant and light, for both single and double action firing; this may become standard for Smith & Wesson and other manufacturers in the future.

There have been other company innovations recently. One has resulted from the desire among the police for a cartridge more powerful than the 9mm but retaining its advantages of penetration and a size allowing a double column magazine. This led to Smith & Wesson's designing a new cartridge, the .40 S&W, which is now in use by many police departments with Smith & Wesson and other makers of handguns.

Another trend has been toward stainless steel finish, as referred to earlier and also as evidenced by Smith & Wesson's Year 2000 catalog showing only three out of sixty-five revolvers as having a blued finish. More recently, the company brought in the innovation for its ultralightweight revolvers of titanium cylinders and the use of the rare element Scandium to strengthen the aluminum frames. This element was discovered in Scandinavia, hence its name.

Above: Sigma Model SW40F, in .40 S&W caliber, serial no. SGM-0001, the starting number for the first production run of Sigma pistols. The Polymer-framed Sigma was introduced in 1994, in part as a response to the emerging popularity of the Glock in the police market. (Courtesy Jim Supica.)

CONTINUED DIVERSIFICATION AND INNOVATION

To understand what Smith & Wesson is doing and producing now and its future prospects, it is helpful to consider the company's recent history. The modern era of Smith & Wesson may be said to have started when Carl Hellstrom became the company's president in 1946 and oversaw the building of a new factory with modern production methods. Smith & Wesson then became dominant over Colt in the supply of firearms for police use, which, together with the military in wartime, is the largest market for handguns. Following Hellstrom's sudden death in 1963, the company continued to expand, but so did the competition, such as Ruger, bringing in new materials and methods of production.

Starting in 1965 the company went through several ownerships by large conglomerates until in 1987 it was purchased by Tomkins plc of England, a large manufacturing and engineering firm. Robert Muddimer, the Tomkins divisional director who became the new Smith & Wesson board chairman, undertook a $5 million capital improvement program (now up to $40 million) to improve quality as well as upgrading and modernizing the company's equipment. However, the company could not keep up with the new trend toward automatics and lost half its market share between 1982 and 1992. Between 1992 and 1994, under president Ed Schultz, the modernization program was completed and the company regained its traditional market share, estimated at 20 percent of total worldwide handgun production.

The components of the company's modern production methods are so up to date that contract services are offered to other companies in metalworking such as in forging and pressing, heat treating, and cutter tool manufacturing and regrinding. The company recently entered into a multi-million dollar, three-year agreement with the Remingon Arms Corp. to produce machined receivers for some of Remington's centerfire rifles.

One important component of this modernization is the installation of computer numerically controlled (CNC) machine tools. An example is described by Charles Petty in a 1994 article in *Guns Magazine*:

"(Revolver) cylinders used to be made in a lengthy process that involved a total of 115 machines performing a total of 94 separate operations. Most were old lathes and milling machines that were dedicated to a single operation. The entire revolver cylinder was re-engineered to be made on modern machines and the end result is that one Computer Numerically Controlled lathe and one CNC machine center have taken the place of those 115 older machines. Tolerances that were once held to thousandths of an inch are now measured in 10 thousandths on a real-time statistical process control computer."

Another component of Smith & Wesson's modern manufacturing process is the use of teams called "businesses" or "cells" making specific parts, instead of the old system of shop foremen and general foremen. This puts more responsibility on individual workers, who are no longer on a piecework basis, and also allows the Japanese system of "on time" production where the movement of materials and parts is closely scheduled.

The company still makes its frames and other major components by forging rather than by casting as done by some other makers, claiming that the parts are stronger this way. The final fitting by skilled gunsmiths has been retained, as has been a rigorous course of test firing for each pistol sold. In 1993, Smith & Wesson was the first American firearms manufacturer to be certified by the International Organization for Standardization (ISO) and still undergoes

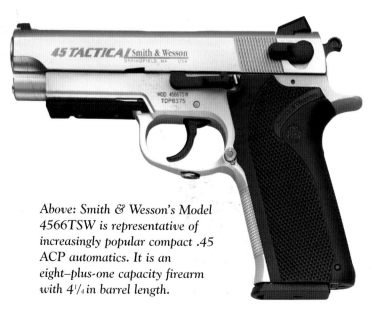

Above: Smith & Wesson's Model 4566TSW is representative of increasingly popular compact .45 ACP automatics. It is an eight–plus-one capacity firearm with 4¹/₄ in barrel length.

Note: the publishers are grateful to Smith & Wesson for permitting reproduction of photographs from the company's 2002 catalog.

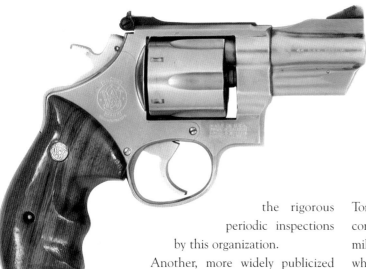

Left: Among the small, concealable, self-defense firearms that have become increasingly available is this S&W Model 624 "Horton Special" revolver, in .44in caliber and with 3in barrel. The weapon's first production run ended in 1958, but it was re-introduced in 1983 and an initial run of 7,500 was sold-out within months. A special chrome-plated version was put into production in 1985 to meet an order from a Massachusetts gun distributor, Lew Horton, following which the weapon was known as the "Horton Special."

the rigorous periodic inspections by this organization.

Another, more widely publicized aspect of the company's recent history has been how the political process and changes in the gun laws have affected Smith & Wesson, as the most visible and widely known handgun maker, more than any of its competitors. At first the effect was in changing the kinds of handguns made. In the United States, the Crime Bill of 1994 restricted the sale of pistol magazines to those having only a 10-round capacity. This increased the market for revolvers, and also produced a new market for .45 ACP automatics since the larger cartridge size was no longer a disadvantage. Also, a number of states passed "right to carry" laws, encouraging individuals to carry handguns for personal defense, adding to the market for small, concealable models.

The next development, however, was less favorable to the company and other gun makers. This was a wave of thirty-two lawsuits brought by cities and counties and by the Federal Government, with the Department of Housing and Urban Development (HUD) as the lead agency, holding Smith & Wesson and other gun makers responsible for deaths and injuries from "gun violence." Fearing that the cost of defending these suits would put it out of business, Smith & Wesson made an agreement with President Clinton's administration undertaking to provide built-in trigger locks and hidden identification numbers, restricting sales at gun shows, and working toward selling only "smart guns" designed to prevent all but the owner from firing the weapon (a technology yet to be proven). In return, the government in thirteen cities agreed to drop their suits for damages against the company.

The backlash from the firearms community and the National Rifle Association was immediate. After the signing of the agreement in March 2000, there was an outcry for a boycott against the company's products, resulting in a 50 percent drop in sales and the laying off of 15 percent of the company's employees, leaving a work force of 525 (in 1994 there were 1,500 workers, but the decrease since then has been partly due to more efficient machine tools and methods of production). Then, in May 2001, the parent company

Tomkins plc sold the company to Saf-T-Hammer, a small company based in Scottsdale, Arizona, for the price of $15 million in cash and a repayment of a $30 million loan – a loss when compared with the $112.5 million it had paid for Smith & Wesson in 1987. Tomkins announced at the time of the sale that this was part of an overall group and product range restructuring.

This new development appears to have been very positive for Smith & Wesson. The president of Saf-T-Hammer and now of the combined company, Robert L. Scott, a former vice president and head of marketing for Smith & Wesson, expresses great pride in returning what he refers to as "this storied company" to American ownership. The present officers of the company do not take responsibility for the March 2000 agreement with the Clinton administration, and the Bush administration has backed off from enforcing it. The threat of litigation has eased: in October 2001 the U.S. Supreme Court decided not to overturn a lower court ruling upholding a State of Louisiana law blocking the city of New Orleans from suing gun manufacturers. Twenty-six other States have passed similar laws.

In terms of Smith & Wesson's sales and profitability, there was a sudden reversal in the downward trend in handgun sales as a result of the September 11, 2001, terrorist attacks on American homeland targets. While chief financial officer John Kelley stated, "It's not the way we would have wanted to do it," the company reported $7.6 million in sales in October, 2001, the month following the attack, and a net profit of $663,000, as compared with a $2 million loss in October 2000.

150th anniversary product range

On that positive note, a look at the Year 2002 company catalog hailing the company's 150th anniversary affords us an insight to what was offered and how the different handgun models related to those described historically in the preceding chapters. The lineup was impressive: fifty different revolvers and fifty-one automatics, ranging from .22in caliber to the .44in Magnum. Six revolvers and two automatics were new for 2002. Four of the revolvers, differing in shape and size, were compact lightweight models with barrels in the 2in range and frames with scandium, a Smith & Wesson innovation introduced in 2002: this is a rare element which when added to aluminum produces a strong lightweight alloy. A revolver called the Model 625 Classic Hunter was offered in the traditional .45 ACP, with 4in barrel and six-round capacity. A new large-frame revolver, Model 629 Classic, was offered in .44 Magnum and .44 S&W Special cartridges, in stainless steel with a satin finish. The two automatics are in traditional double action, for 9mm and .40 S&W cartridges, respectively. All of these new revolvers and automatics are fitted with "Light Gathering HIVIZ" sights, with an orange dot on the front sight and adjustable rear sights.

Six revolvers were offered in .22in caliber and in stainless steel. Frame sizes range from small to medium, and there are both six-round and ten-round cylinders. Eight AirLite revolvers were listed with aluminum alloy frames and titanium cylinders, for .32 Magnum, .38 S&W, .39 S&W Special plus P, and .44 S&W Special cartridges. Seven more AirLite revolvers were shown with the scandium alloy frames, using the .357 Magnum cartridge. Of the latter fifteen revolvers mentioned, five had the letters "PD" attached to the model numbers, reflecting their design for police use.

The catalog showed a group of five Airweight compact revolvers with aluminum frames and cylinders and barrels of stainless steel, designed for a lower price range, and including the Chiefs Special configuration introduced in 1952. There was an additional group of four small frame revolvers in .357 Magnum with construction of stainless steel, including a Chiefs Special, and also a hammerless Bodyguard model.

The next group shown in the catalog included fifteen medium frame revolvers using the .38 S&W Special, the .38 Special Plus P, the .357 Magnum, and the .44 S&W Special cartridges. The most popular was shown as the Model 686, in .357 Magnum, with a choice of six- or seven-round

cylinders. These are all descendants of the original .38 S&W Special Military and Police revolver introduced in 1899. An interesting feature is that all current revolvers have rubber grips by Hogue, except for the LadySmiths.

Eight large frame stainless steel revolvers were also shown, including five in the original "Dirty Harry" .44 Magnum. One of these had the special feature of the PowerPort, which is a cut in the barrel just behind the muzzle allowing gas to escape and reducing recoil. The other three revolvers in this group were in 10mm, .45 ACP, and .41 Magnum calibers.

Of the six LadySmith handguns shown, five were small and medium frame revolvers, while the other was a compact 9mm pistol, "all designed for the discriminating female shooter." The calibers ranged from .22in to .357 Magnum for the revolvers, and 9mm for the compact automatic. Deluxe cases were also offered for the LadySmith revolvers.

In Smith & Wesson's 2002 automatic pistol product line, there were shown eight automatics using the .22in rimfire cartridge. Configurations varied from a compact 4in barrel to a 7in barrel target model, and a 5½in model with a heavy "bull" barrel. The pistols were described as meeting "the demands of the competitor and the expectations of the weekend plinker," reflecting their expected use.

Three Chiefs Special compact automatics were included in the catalog. They were in aluminum alloy/stainless steel, in 9mm, .40 S&W, and .45 ACP calibers. These again are designed for the traditional use of police officers required to carry sidearms but not on patrol, as well as for self-defense and for use by bodyguards. Six compact automatics made up the Value Series, again for law enforcement back-up and concealed-carry applications. Three of these were in 9mm caliber, reflecting common police use; two were in .40 S&W, a more advanced police application, and one is in the traditional .45 ACP.

The TSW Series of fifteen automatics presented, referring to "tactical" law enforcement use, were described as Smith & Wesson's premier metal pistol line. They featured aluminum and steel frames, and ranged in caliber from 9mm to .40 S&W and .45 ACP. These models had the added features of an equipment rail, magazine disconnect, loaded chamber indicator and Novak Lo-Mount Carry sights, and were shown to be available in compact and full sized models. The equipment rail is for a high power flashlight attachment or a laser sight, which projects a red dot on the intended target. The latter is an innovation which increases accuracy by showing exactly where the bullet will go, and occasionally has had the effect of encouraging perpetrators to surrender to the police when they see that they are "marked" with the red dot; but the device has the disadvantage that the location of the shooter

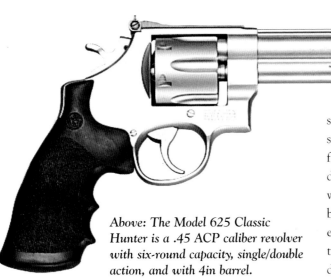

Above: The Model 625 Classic Hunter is a .45 ACP caliber revolver with six-round capacity, single/double action, and with 4in barrel.

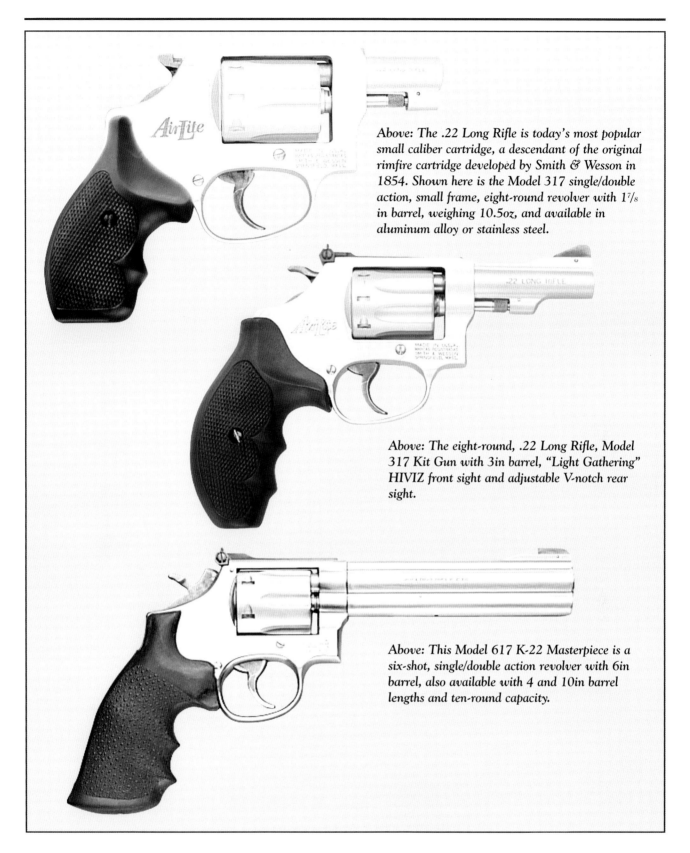

Above: The .22 Long Rifle is today's most popular small caliber cartridge, a descendant of the original rimfire cartridge developed by Smith & Wesson in 1854. Shown here is the Model 317 single/double action, small frame, eight-round revolver with 1⁷/₈ in barrel, weighing 10.5oz, and available in aluminum alloy or stainless steel.

Above: The eight-round, .22 Long Rifle, Model 317 Kit Gun with 3in barrel, "Light Gathering" HIVIZ front sight and adjustable V-notch rear sight.

Above: This Model 617 K-22 Masterpiece is a six-shot, single/double action revolver with 6in barrel, also available with 4 and 10in barrel lengths and ten-round capacity.

is more easily seen by opponents.

There were seven variations of the Sigma polymer frame and steel slide pistol in the Year 2002 catalog. This firearm was introduced by Smith & Wesson in 1994, in response to the popularity with police departments of the Glock line. These pistols are in double action only with no manual safety, so that the action of the trigger is immediately available for firing at all times. The trigger pull is relatively hard, which minimizes the danger of accidental firing if

dropped. The pistol is adaptable to a double column magazine design allowing a capacity of up to seventeen rounds, but under U.S. law such weapons can be sold only for law enforcement use and for export, with only the standard eleven-round magazine being allowed to be sold commercially in the United States. Unlike the other Smith & Wesson handguns, only the barrel and slide are made by the company itself, the rest of the components being made by outside suppliers.

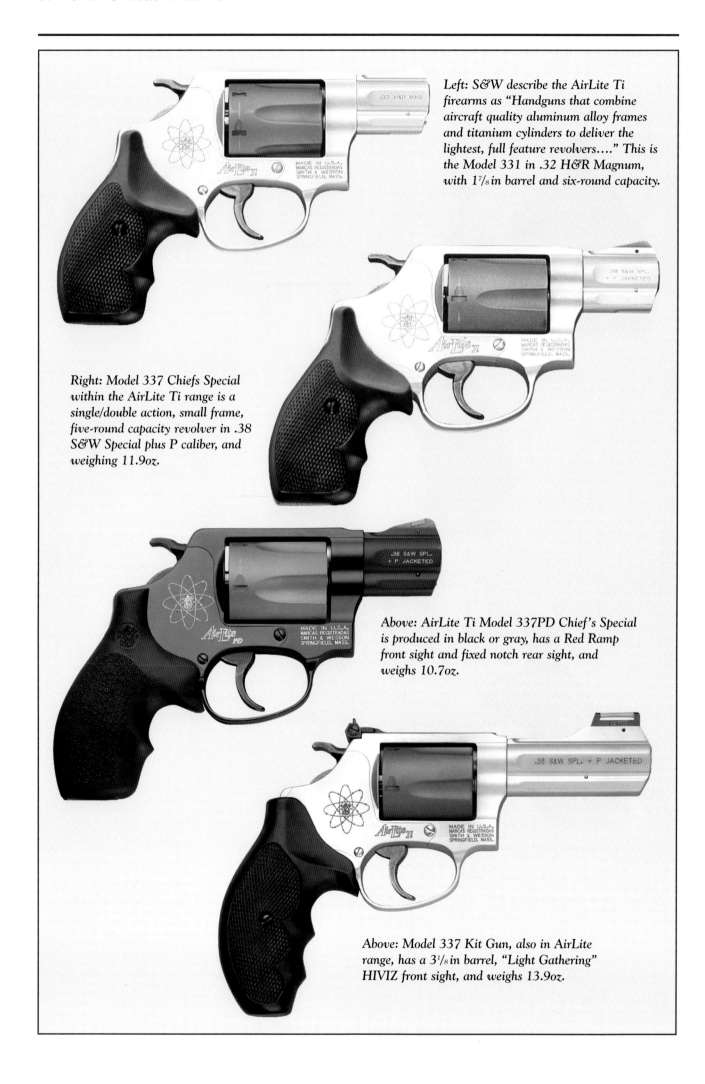

Left: S&W describe the AirLite Ti firearms as "Handguns that combine aircraft quality aluminum alloy frames and titanium cylinders to deliver the lightest, full feature revolvers...." This is the Model 331 in .32 H&R Magnum, with 1⁷/₈ in barrel and six-round capacity.

Right: Model 337 Chiefs Special within the AirLite Ti range is a single/double action, small frame, five-round capacity revolver in .38 S&W Special plus P caliber, and weighing 11.9oz.

Above: AirLite Ti Model 337PD Chief's Special is produced in black or gray, has a Red Ramp front sight and fixed notch rear sight, and weighs 10.7oz.

Above: Model 337 Kit Gun, also in AirLite range, has a 3¹/₈ in barrel, "Light Gathering" HIVIZ front sight, and weighs 13.9oz.

Two variations of the SW99 Series automatic were also shown in the catalog. This firearm was designed and produced in collaboration with Walther. The latter makes all the components except for the barrel and slide. Of traditional double action for the first shot and single action after that, this model has the special features of a visible indicator when the chamber is loaded, a red-tipped indicator protruding from the rear of the slide indicating when the striker is cocked and the pistol is ready to fire, a decocking button on the top left side of the slide, and an ambidextrous magazine release at the bottom rear of the trigger guard. The construction is polymer with a steel barrel and slide, and the model is made in 9mm and .40 S&W.

Smith & Wesson's Performance Center, initiated in 1991, is a special shop outside the main factory devoted to providing special features (customers could order their own designs or features to be made) and for making limited-run specialties such as for Olympic competition and for the

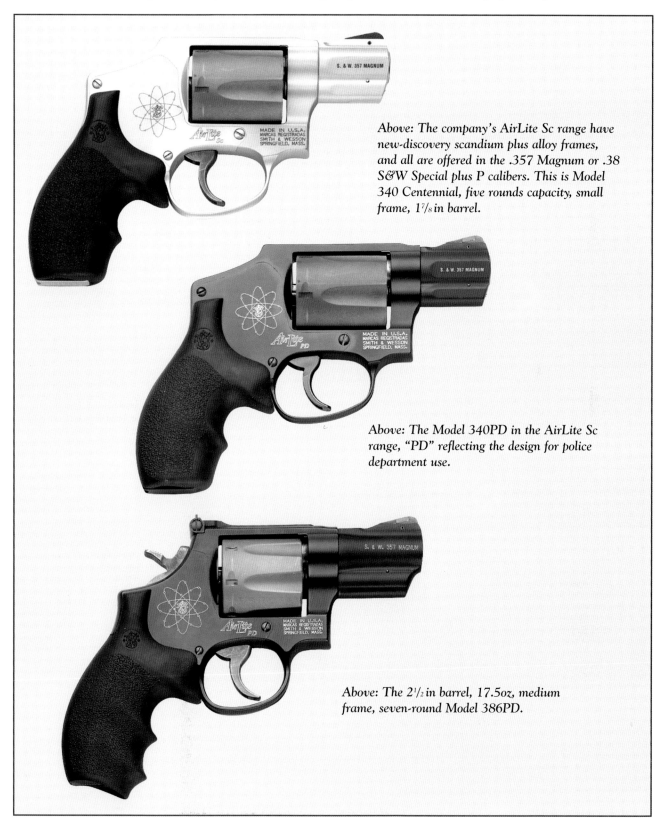

Above: The company's AirLite Sc range have new-discovery scandium plus alloy frames, and all are offered in the .357 Magnum or .38 S&W Special plus P calibers. This is Model 340 Centennial, five rounds capacity, small frame, $1^7/_8$ in barrel.

Above: The Model 340PD in the AirLite Sc range, "PD" reflecting the design for police department use.

Above: The $2^1/_2$ in barrel, 17.5oz, medium frame, seven-round Model 386PD.

Smith & Wesson shooting team of company representatives who enter worldwide competitions. For the first time, in 2002 the Performance Center began selling directly to the public instead of to distributors, with three models available: the Model 627 revolver in .357 Magnum and .38 S&W Special plus P with a contoured barrel and other special features; the Model 952 Automatic 9mm with wood grips and a hammer block safety system independent of trigger pull; and a reproduction of the original Model 3 Schofield top-break Army revolver, with a .45 S&W Schofield cartridge (several other companies also make Schofield reproductions). The Schofield reproduction is in response for the growing popularity of the sport of Cowboy Action Shooting, in which original Old West arms or replicas are

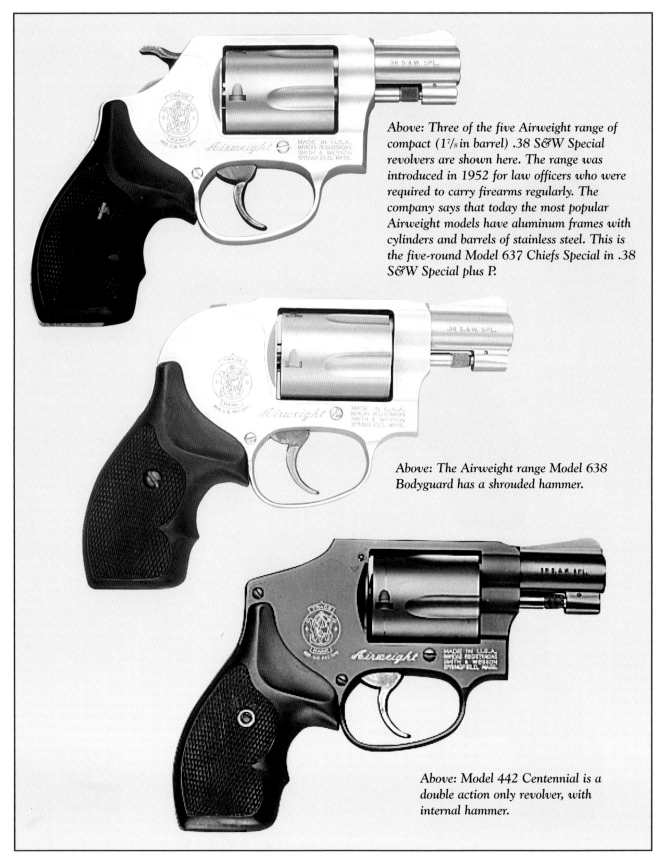

Above: Three of the five Airweight range of compact (1⁷/₈ in barrel) .38 S&W Special revolvers are shown here. The range was introduced in 1952 for law officers who were required to carry firearms regularly. The company says that today the most popular Airweight models have aluminum frames with cylinders and barrels of stainless steel. This is the five-round Model 637 Chiefs Special in .38 S&W Special plus P.

Above: The Airweight range Model 638 Bodyguard has a shrouded hammer.

Above: Model 442 Centennial is a double action only revolver, with internal hammer.

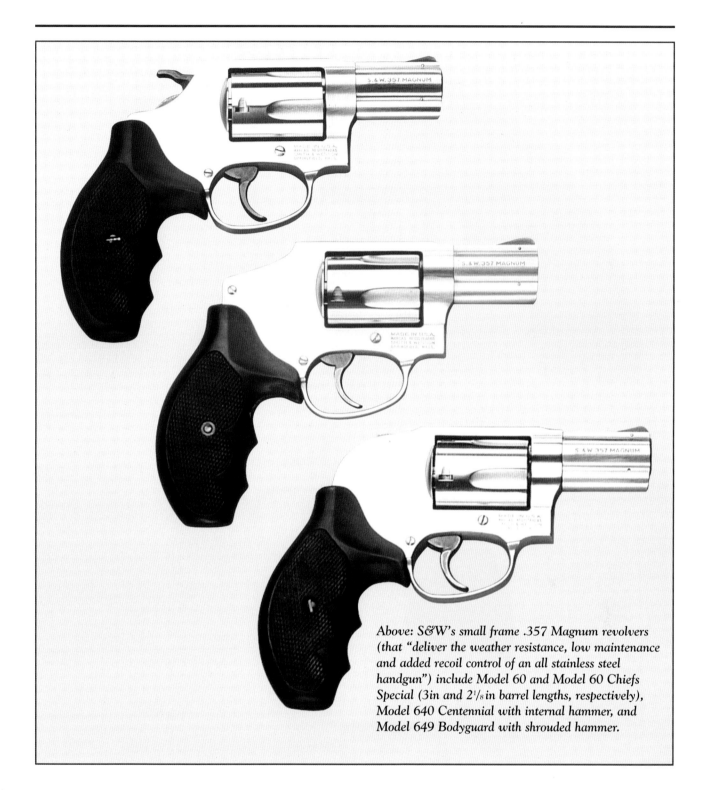

Above: S&W's small frame .357 Magnum revolvers (that "deliver the weather resistance, low maintenance and added recoil control of an all stainless steel handgun") include Model 60 and Model 60 Chiefs Special (3in and 2⅛in barrel lengths, respectively), Model 640 Centennial with internal hammer, and Model 649 Bodyguard with shrouded hammer.

used and the participants even dress in Old West costume. The Performance Center also offers general gunsmithing services for Smith & Wesson handguns, laser engraving, and special grips which can be provided with inlaid picture designs.

Security innovations brought in by the Saf-T-Hammer company include triggerguards equipped with buttons operated by a special key, blocking the trigger when in a raised position. This was a major product of the company before it acquired Smith & Wesson, along with the "Shockproof Security Cable" for guns and the "Versa Vault" case for gun storage, of cast aluminum and steel construction, opening by means of a lighted keypad with four keys.

As an additional service for its customers, the company provides an extensive, modern Shooting Sports Center near its Springfield plant. Here there are multiple civilian training ranges, a twenty-lane rental range, classrooms. a museum and a student lounge. On a recent visit to Springfield the writer had an opportunity to visit the Center and also to observe the 2002 Winter Championships of the International Defensive Pistol Association (IDPA). This is a regular a three-day event with competitions, tours of the plant and the Springfield Armory, and a reception and dinner. In the 2002 competition there were nine "stages" of the type similar to those used for training the police and military, with the participant moving through several stations and firing at moving targets representing

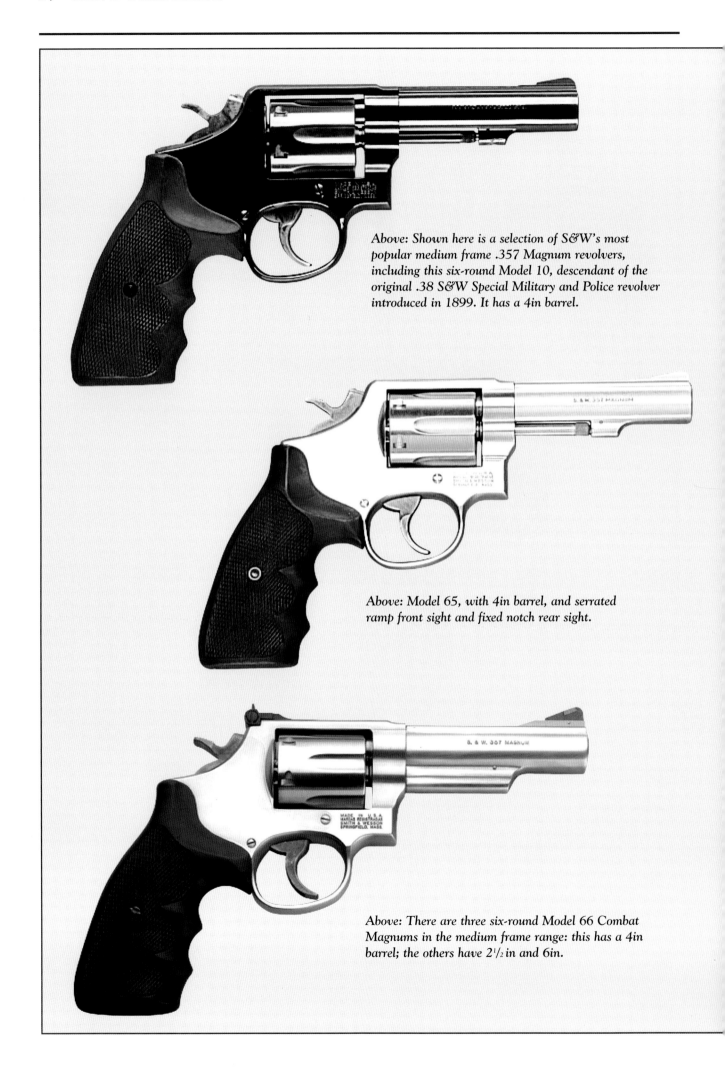

Above: Shown here is a selection of S&W's most popular medium frame .357 Magnum revolvers, including this six-round Model 10, descendant of the original .38 S&W Special Military and Police revolver introduced in 1899. It has a 4in barrel.

Above: Model 65, with 4in barrel, and serrated ramp front sight and fixed notch rear sight.

Above: There are three six-round Model 66 Combat Magnums in the medium frame range: this has a 4in barrel; the others have 2½in and 6in.

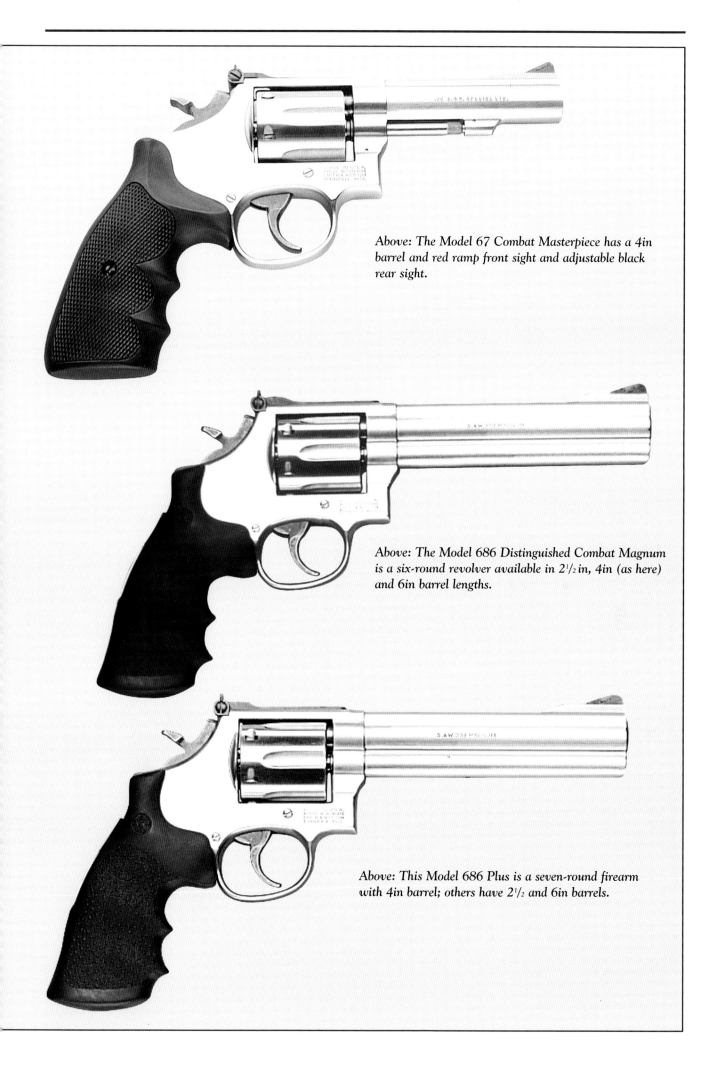

Above: The Model 67 Combat Masterpiece has a 4in barrel and red ramp front sight and adjustable black rear sight.

Above: The Model 686 Distinguished Combat Magnum is a six-round revolver available in 2¹/₂in, 4in (as here) and 6in barrel lengths.

Above: This Model 686 Plus is a seven-round firearm with 4in barrel; others have 2¹/₂ and 6in barrels.

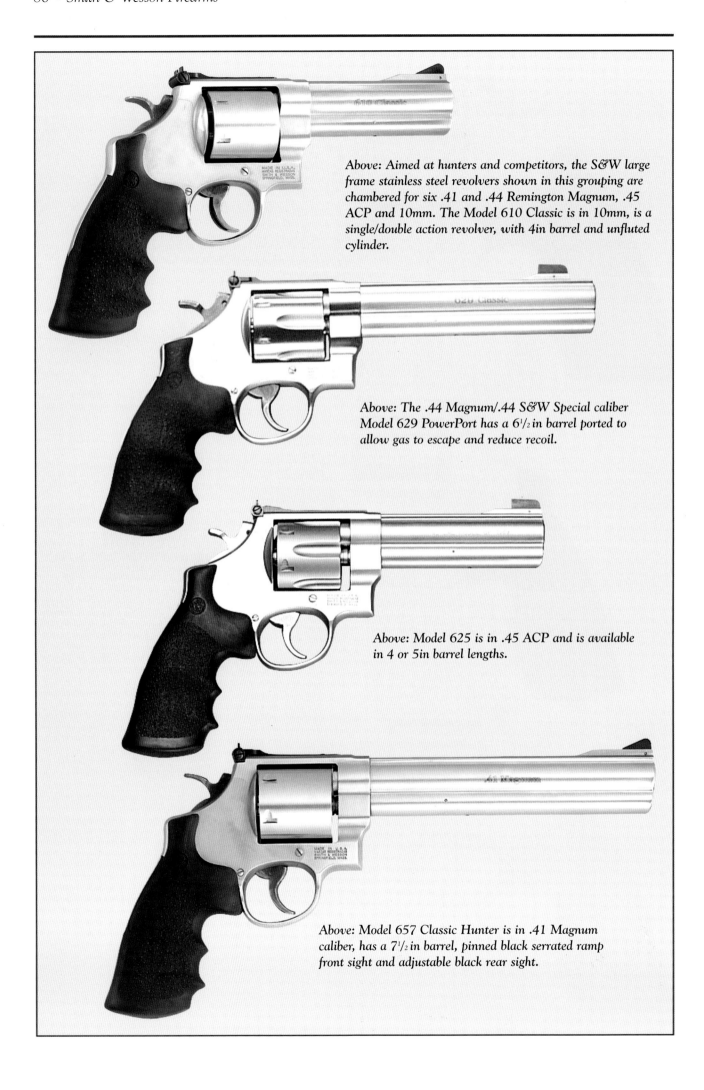

Above: Aimed at hunters and competitors, the S&W large frame stainless steel revolvers shown in this grouping are chambered for six .41 and .44 Remington Magnum, .45 ACP and 10mm. The Model 610 Classic is in 10mm, is a single/double action revolver, with 4in barrel and unfluted cylinder.

Above: The .44 Magnum/.44 S&W Special caliber Model 629 PowerPort has a 6½ in barrel ported to allow gas to escape and reduce recoil.

Above: Model 625 is in .45 ACP and is available in 4 or 5in barrel lengths.

Above: Model 657 Classic Hunter is in .41 Magnum caliber, has a 7½ in barrel, pinned black serrated ramp front sight and adjustable black rear sight.

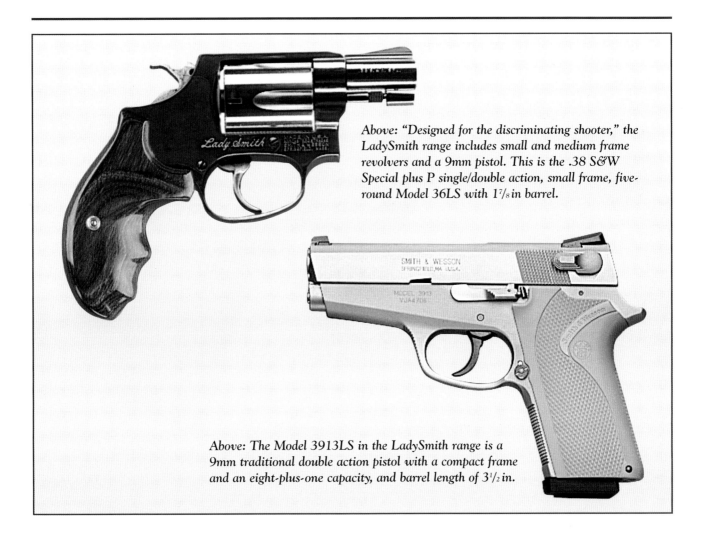

Above: "Designed for the discriminating shooter," the LadySmith range includes small and medium frame revolvers and a 9mm pistol. This is the .38 S&W Special plus P single/double action, small frame, five-round Model 36LS with 1⁷/₈ in barrel.

Above: The Model 3913LS in the LadySmith range is a 9mm traditional double action pistol with a compact frame and an eight-plus-one capacity, and barrel length of 3¹/₂ in.

perpetrators interspersed with no-shoot targets, such as of a bystander instead of a perpetrator.

The facilities used are part of the Smith & Wesson Academy, which is the oldest private training facility for law enforcement in the United States. Participants come from all over the nation and from overseas to be trained in the use and maintenance of firearms. Training facilities are also available for gunsmithing, involving the repair and maintenance of Smith & Wesson arms. The rental ranges are open to the public, and attract handgun enthusiasts from a wide surrounding area.

In the period since World War II the company has developed a line of franchised products related to shooting sports, such as clothing and watches, using the Smith & Wesson logo. This has now reached the point where the company operates four retail stores, one adjacent to the Shooting Sports Center in Springfield and others in Myrtle Beach, South Carolina, Branson, Missouri, and East Pigeon Forge, Tennessee. Recently the company has started manufacturing mountain bicycles especially designed for the police, and these are on sale at the retail stores. However, having learned its lesson in the 1920s, the company has not gone into the manufacture of unrelated items as it did then, such as razor blade savers and toilet flush valves!

The outlook for the immediate future is reasonably promising. Based on the company's profitability regained

after September 11, 2001, at the time of this writing the company's stock has advanced from $0.75 in early 2001 to over $1. However, the future of the civilian market at least could be clouded by the antigun legislation backed by organizations like Handgun Control Inc. The Clinton

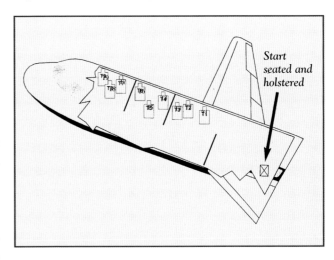

Start seated and holstered

Above: At S&W's Shooting Sports Center the 2002 Winter Championships of the International Defensive Pistol Association included as Stage 1 this "Sky Marshal Rescue" event where the competitor had to thwart a hijacking, beginning as if seated in the "coach" section of the airliner and engaging the targets (T1 to T9) in first class and galley sections in stages, using the walls (bold straight lines) as cover.

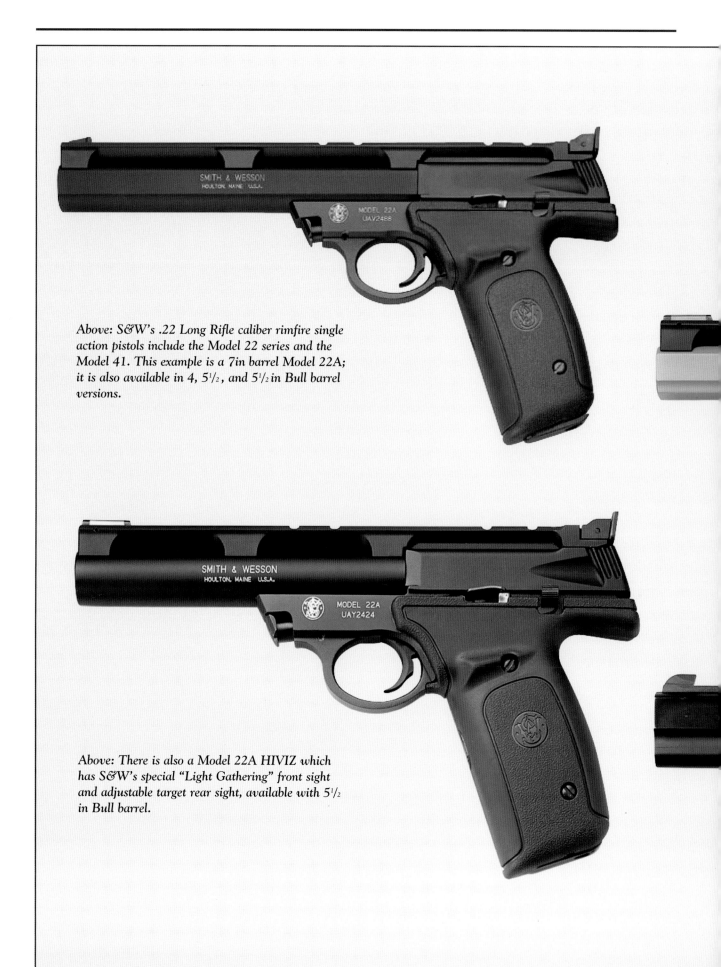

Above: S&W's .22 Long Rifle caliber rimfire single action pistols include the Model 22 series and the Model 41. This example is a 7in barrel Model 22A; it is also available in 4, 5¹/₂, and 5¹/₂ in Bull barrel versions.

Above: There is also a Model 22A HIVIZ which has S&W's special "Light Gathering" front sight and adjustable target rear sight, available with 5¹/₂ in Bull barrel.

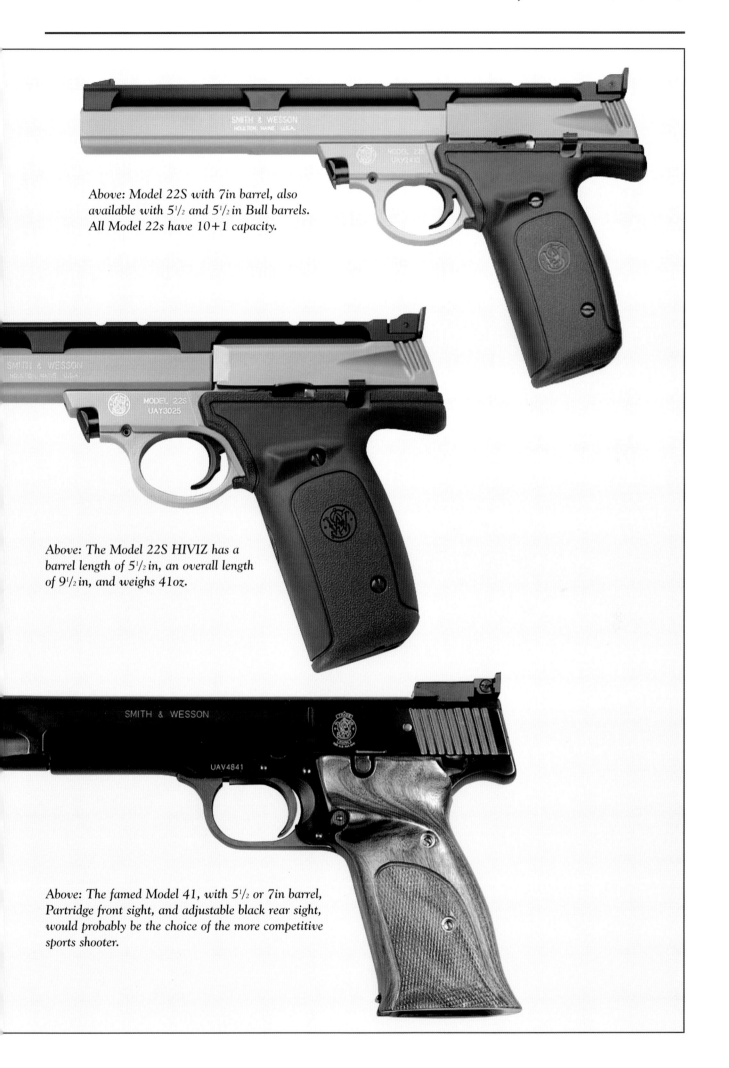

Above: Model 22S with 7in barrel, also available with 5½ and 5½ in Bull barrels. All Model 22s have 10+1 capacity.

Above: The Model 22S HIVIZ has a barrel length of 5½ in, an overall length of 9½ in, and weighs 41oz.

Above: The famed Model 41, with 5½ or 7in barrel, Partridge front sight, and adjustable black rear sight, would probably be the choice of the more competitive sports shooter.

administration, as well as bringing a suit as described above against handgun manufacturers, also supported a series of bills in Congress to restrict and potentially confiscate all handguns, as has been done in Britain, Australia, and several other countries. The present Bush administration has sided with those opposing these efforts, and none of the proposed restrictive new laws has proceeded toward Congressional approval. At the time of this writing, the visibility of the antigun movement, with its "Mothers Marches" and other forms of protest, has subsided. There is more recognition of the need for self-defense after September 11, 2001, and

there have been calls, for example, for the arming of airline pilots and for having armed anti-terrorist specialists aboard airliners. However, there is always the possibility of shootings by demented persons with attendant publicity, such as the assassination attempt on Ronald Reagan and the shootings at Columbine High School, which could revive the antigun movement.

Handgun sales are already strictly regulated in the United States under the 1992 Brady Bill. All firearms dealers must be licensed, and any firearms purchase transaction requires a Federal background check and payment of a fee. There is no

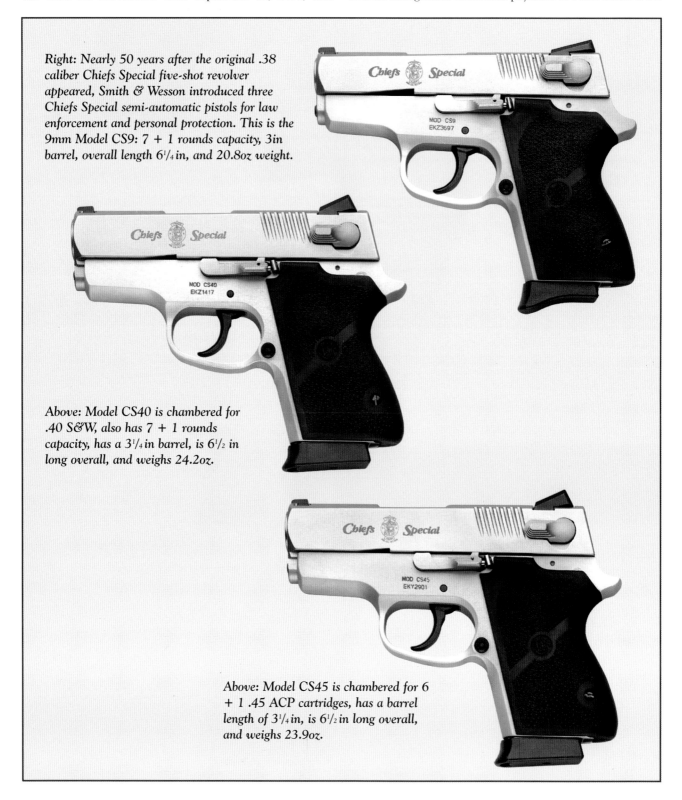

Right: Nearly 50 years after the original .38 caliber Chiefs Special five-shot revolver appeared, Smith & Wesson introduced three Chiefs Special semi-automatic pistols for law enforcement and personal protection. This is the 9mm Model CS9: 7 + 1 rounds capacity, 3in barrel, overall length 6¼in, and 20.8oz weight.

Above: Model CS40 is chambered for .40 S&W, also has 7 + 1 rounds capacity, has a 3¼in barrel, is 6½in long overall, and weighs 24.2oz.

Above: Model CS45 is chambered for 6 + 1 .45 ACP cartridges, has a barrel length of 3¼in, is 6½in long overall, and weighs 23.9oz.

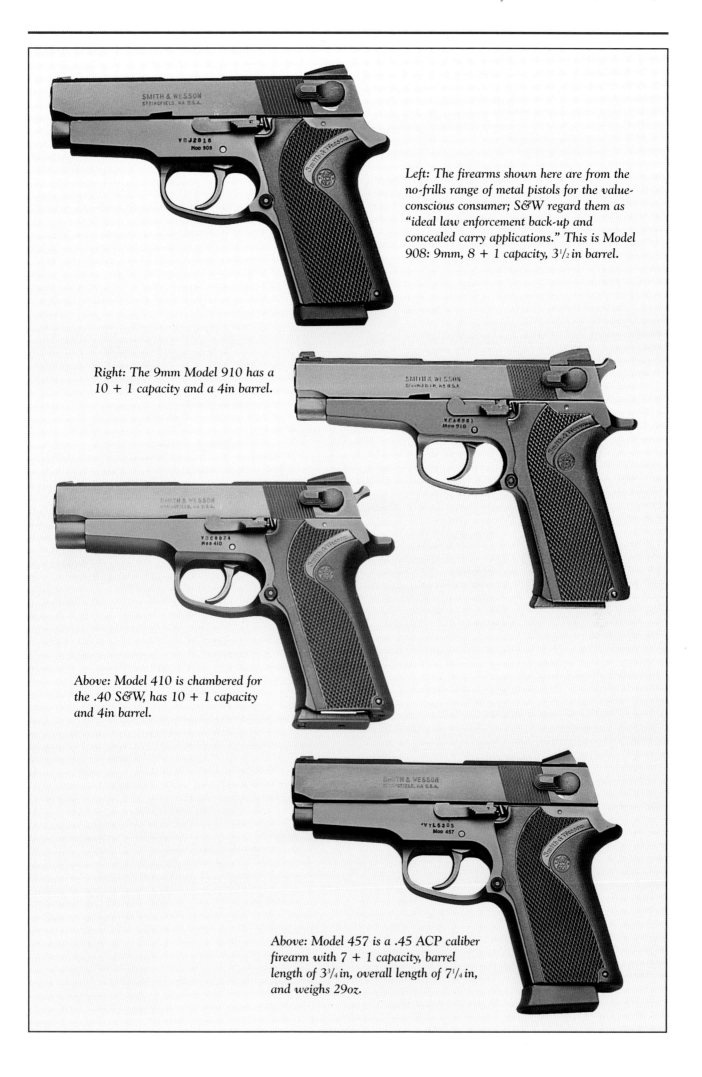

Left: The firearms shown here are from the no-frills range of metal pistols for the value-conscious consumer; S&W regard them as "ideal law enforcement back-up and concealed carry applications." This is Model 908: 9mm, 8 + 1 capacity, 3½ in barrel.

Right: The 9mm Model 910 has a 10 + 1 capacity and a 4in barrel.

Above: Model 410 is chambered for the .40 S&W, has 10 + 1 capacity and 4in barrel.

Above: Model 457 is a .45 ACP caliber firearm with 7 + 1 capacity, barrel length of 3¾ in, overall length of 7¼ in, and weighs 29oz.

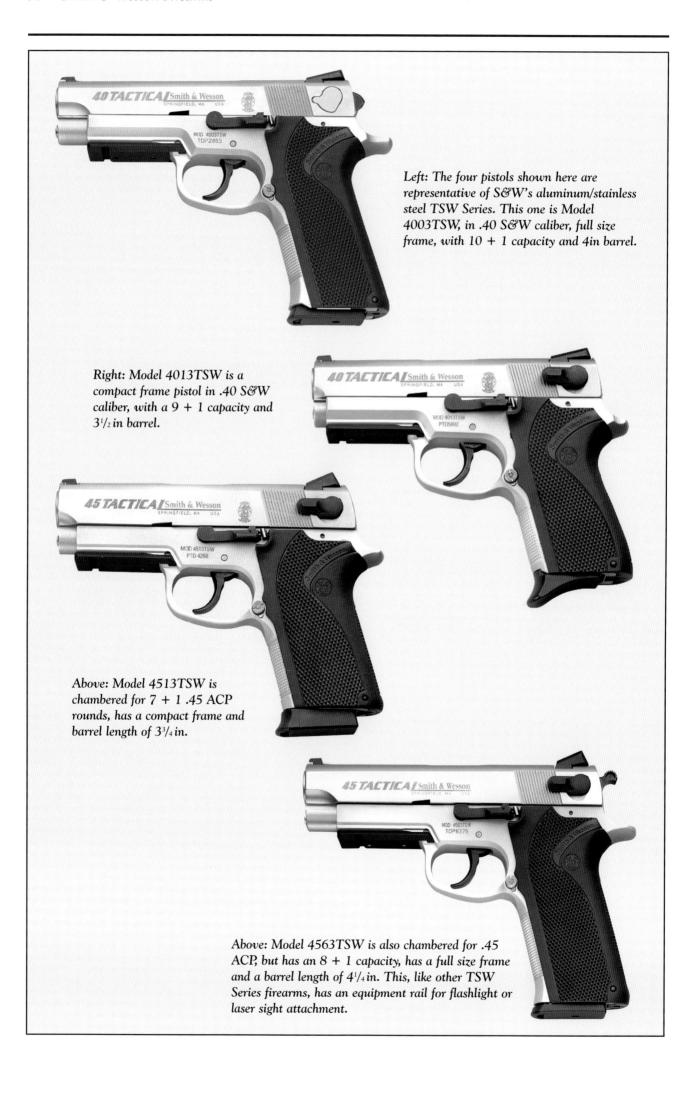

Left: The four pistols shown here are representative of S&W's aluminum/stainless steel TSW Series. This one is Model 4003TSW, in .40 S&W caliber, full size frame, with 10 + 1 capacity and 4in barrel.

Right: Model 4013TSW is a compact frame pistol in .40 S&W caliber, with a 9 + 1 capacity and 3$^{1}/_{2}$ in barrel.

Above: Model 4513TSW is chambered for 7 + 1 .45 ACP rounds, has a compact frame and barrel length of 3$^{3}/_{4}$ in.

Above: Model 4563TSW is also chambered for .45 ACP, but has an 8 + 1 capacity, has a full size frame and a barrel length of 4$^{1}/_{4}$ in. This, like other TSW Series firearms, has an equipment rail for flashlight or laser sight attachment.

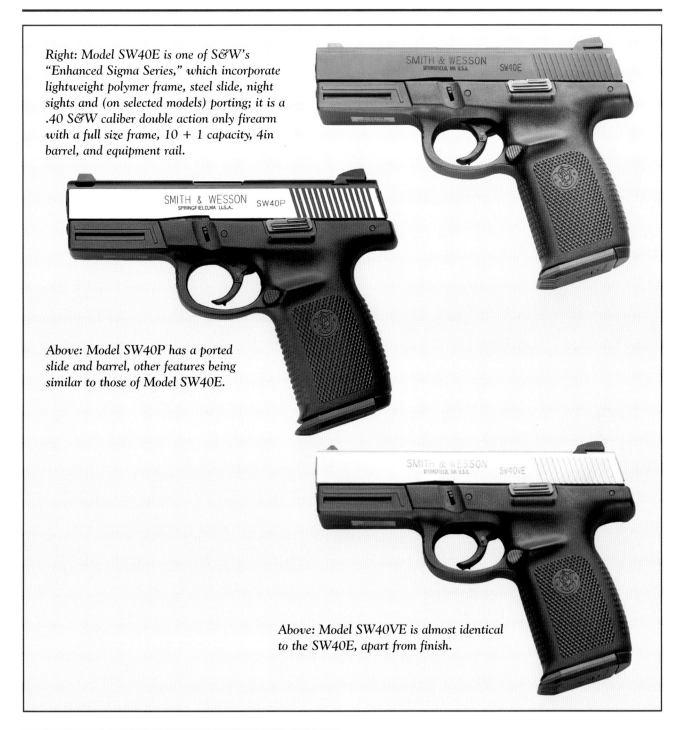

Right: Model SW40E is one of S&W's "Enhanced Sigma Series," which incorporate lightweight polymer frame, steel slide, night sights and (on selected models) porting; it is a .40 S&W caliber double action only firearm with a full size frame, 10 + 1 capacity, 4in barrel, and equipment rail.

Above: Model SW40P has a ported slide and barrel, other features being similar to those of Model SW40E.

Above: Model SW40VE is almost identical to the SW40E, apart from finish.

"gun show loophole" for handguns; any purchase must be from a licensed dealer, with a background check. Also, the Federal Bureau of Alcohol, Tobacco, and Firearms has a program, with extra agents assigned, to check on the few dealers who sell most of the guns used in crimes, and some cities and states have adopted the Project Exile program begun in Richmond, Virginia, under which perpetrators using guns in committing crimes automatically receive

Left: Seconds after President Ronald Reagan waved to the crowd outside the Capitol Hilton, March 30, 1981, he and Press Secretary James Brady (dark suit, behind Reagan's arm) and Officer Thomas Delahanty (left of umbrella) were hit by an attempted assassin's bullets. Such incidents have brought pressure for more gun control. (Photo Michael Evans, courtesy The White House.)

Federal jail sentences. In addition, the National Rifle Association has had substantial success in its "Eddie Eagle GunSafe Program" of warning schoolchildren to stay away from and report any handguns they may find.

Perhaps the most insidious of the bills which have been introduced in Congress, from the viewpoint of handgun owners, would have the government maintain a permanent record of all handgun purchasers; the present Brady Bill prohibits such records being kept for more than a short time. In the countries which have made handguns illegal, such registries were used to make owners turn them in; and the sponsors of this proposal may well intend to follow the same procedure in the United States. Other bills are more extreme, and their approval is difficult to foresee: raising the taxes on handguns and ammunition by 1,000 percent,

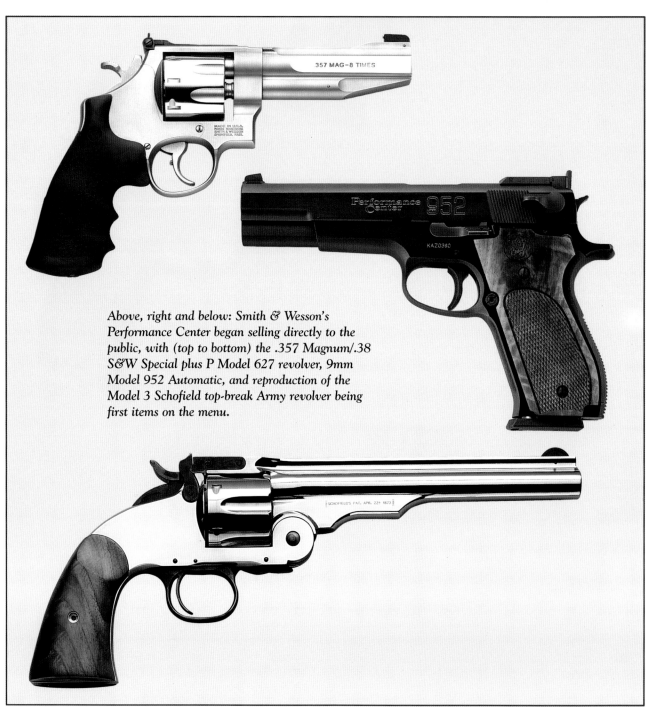

Above, right and below: Smith & Wesson's Performance Center began selling directly to the public, with (top to bottom) the .357 Magnum/.38 S&W Special plus P Model 627 revolver, 9mm Model 952 Automatic, and reproduction of the Model 3 Schofield top-break Army revolver being first items on the menu.

Above and left: The FBI and police departments have rigorous training regimes, as does Smith & Wesson at its Academy. There are those who would argue that the only carriers and users of handguns and some other firearms should be law enforcement officers. (Courtesy Library of Congress.)

obviously intended to discourage such purchases; subsidizing "turn in" programs where owners are paid a nominal amount, which has already been shown to be useless as a crime-fighting tool; and requiring that handguns be fitted with a fingerprint or other identification system such that they can be fired by only one person, a technology that does not exist.

Unfortunately, this issue tends to be debated on the basis of emotion rather than reason, and to the extent that it is a question of public health, as is sometimes contended, there should be objective research as in the case of diseases and other public health threats. In any event, there are reasons, which seem compelling to this writer, against the prohibition of handguns in the United States. The first may be debatable but cannot be ignored under the American system of democratic government: the wording of the U.S. Constitution appears to support the handgunners' side. The Second Amendment of the Bill of Rights states as follows: "A well regulated Militia, being necessary to the security of a free State, that the right of the people to keep and bear Arms shall not be infringed." A Federal Appeals Court judge, Sam R. Cummings, in Texas, ruled in 1999 that this gives

individual citizens the right to own firearms, but opponents claim that the wording refers only to the National Guard and not to individual citizens, which is a dubious claim in this writer's opinion.

Perhaps a more practical reason to keep handguns legal is for self-defense against criminals. Experience in both Britain and Australia has shown a substantial increase in armed robberies and gun-related homicides since their bans went into effect. While probably only a minority of citizens would be prepared to use their handguns against criminals, a situation in which all citizens' handguns are removed, allowing criminals to proceed with impunity, would certainly be dangerous. Also, as took place in the United States in the 1920s with the law prohibiting liquor, there would be a large illicit traffic in guns, which would produce still more crime.

A movement to ban handguns or make their purchase so difficult as to amount to a ban is contrary to the American tradition of shooting sports, including hunting. Rifle and pistol shooting are established sports, with many international competitions, including the Olympic Games. They are also recognized as healthy outdoor sports, not "gun violence."

Finally, and here the writer admits to some bias, unreasonable controls on handgun possession and purchase would stop the hobby of antique gun collecting. This is closely tied in with the appreciation of history. As shown in the preceding chapters of this book, the handgun has been an important element in the settlement of the western part of the United States as well as in its foreign wars and in law enforcement. The collector is induced to become a student of history, and many enthusiasts enjoy taking part in reenactments such as of the Old West and the Civil War. The confiscation of firearms does not discriminate between historic antiques and modern arms.

Right: Pressure for tighter control of gun usage spans many years. Here, in 1975 Mary Singleton, at the time Florida's Democratic representative from Jacksonville, holds a .357 Magnum as she makes a point of comparison before the House Criminal Justice Committee which was considering a bill to outlaw the lighter "Saturday night specials." The bill foundered, apparently because of a general feeling that manufacturers would "find ways around the law even if passed." (Copyright Washington Post; reprinted by permission of the D.C. Public Library.)

COLLECTING, INVESTING AND WHERE TO SEE THE GUNS

The collecting of arms is a centuries-long tradition, as pointed out by firearms author R. L. Wilson, "due to their history, artistry, craftsmanship, mechanics, romance, and performance." The nobility in Europe had private armories, American tycoons like William Randolph Hearst were avid collectors, and noted figures like "Buffalo Bill" Cody prided themselves on their gun collections. Today, probably most of the gun owners in the United States, variously estimated in the television program *Investigative Reports* at 44 million and by the National Rifle Association at 60-65 million, are "collectors" in the sense that they acquire and keep firearms for their inherent interest and value, rather than only as a tool for hunting and target shooting.

A subcategory among firearm collectibles is antique arms, generally defined as being made before the year 1900. *Flayderman's Guide to Antique American Firearms* notes that Smith & Wesson arms have always enjoyed great popularity among collectors. R. L. Wilson estimates that there are 20,000 to 25,000 collectors who specialize in Colts; for Smith & Wesson the number is probably not far behind. This total does not include the many owners of more modern Smith & Wesson handguns who qualify as collectors: for example, one observer has commented that many purchasers of the popular .44 Magnum "Dirty Harry" revolver have hardly ever fired it, but were attracted just by its notoriety and impressive weight and appearance.

The lure of collecting Smith & Wesson firearms is demonstrated by the growth of the Smith & Wesson Collectors' Association (SWCA), started in 1964 as the first of the specialized collector organizations founded in the United States (examples of others include Colt, Winchester, Remington, and Ruger). From a nucleus of six collectors, the SWCA has now grown to a membership of approximately 600. At first holding meetings only in conjunction with established gun shows, the Association now holds its own annual four-day meetings in different parts of the country. These are open only to members, who display and trade their

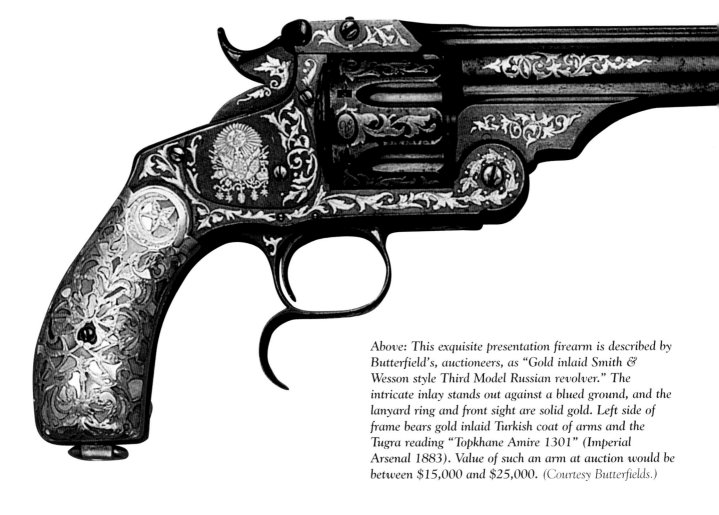

Above: This exquisite presentation firearm is described by Butterfield's, auctioneers, as "Gold inlaid Smith & Wesson style Third Model Russian revolver." The intricate inlay stands out against a blued ground, and the lanyard ring and front sight are solid gold. Left side of frame bears gold inlaid Turkish coat of arms and the Tugra reading "Topkhane Amire 1301" (Imperial Arsenal 1883). Value of such an arm at auction would be between $15,000 and $25,000. (Courtesy Butterfields.)

holdings, participate in educational talks, and take sightseeing trips in the local area. Membership is open only to individuals who are serious Smith & Wesson collectors and are recommended by a present member; those interested can obtain further information about joining from Sheryl Cheely, S&W CA, P.O. 32, Great Bend, KS 67530. No financial aid or special treatment in the purchase of firearms has been asked of the Smith & Wesson Company, so that the organization can remain independent. A periodic newsletter is published, and also the association has provided important financial support for the Connecticut Valley Historical Association, which is now the repository of the company's large collection of its historic arms.

Colt and Winchester may be better known among collectors of antique arms than Smith & Wesson, because both makers produced more guns and in more varieties before the turn of the century. However, early Smith & Wesson handguns have the same historic appeal stemming from the Civil War and the Old West, and after 1900 Smith & Wesson began to outpace Colt and Winchester in the number and variety of arms produced. The Smith & Wesson collector has the advantage that Smith & Wessons are widely distributed, such as in gun shops where antiques are normally not carried, but where older varieties of Smith & Wessons are interspersed with current production handguns. The main obstacle may be the red tape in buying an older

collectible Smith & Wesson, the purchase of which may be treated the same as in buying a new handgun. In New Jersey, for example, the prospective purchaser must first be fingerprinted for a Firearms Identification card, and then for each handgun purchased must obtain a separate permit from the local police department, and including the Federal background check will be required. Antique handguns are treated the same as modern, and only one purchase per two weeks is allowed. Massachusetts has even more stringent requirements, and reports are that purchasers are going to adjoining states to add desirable pieces to their collections.

Such restrictions have reduced the number of gun shops and dealers where collectible (generally those not currently manufactured) Smith & Wessons can be found. However, a number of well-established and reputable dealers in different parts of the country issue catalogs and also hold auctions of fine antique arms. Increasingly, also, these can be seen on the Internet. The gun magazines listed in the bibliography to this book carry advertisements and list auctions held by these dealers.

In addition, gun shows where firearms can be bought are held on a periodic basis all over the United States. These are

---

COLLECTORS' GUN CONDITION GUIDE

The National Rifle Association standards for condition should be kept in mind by collectors, recognizing that the published price guides do not even assign values to specimens in less than "Good" condition, except for the very rarest and valuable. Collectors should avoid such specimens anyway, for safety reasons. "Fine to Excellent" as well as "Factory New" examples command the highest prices and have had the largest rate of increase.

"Factory New" – all original parts; 100 percent original finish; in perfect condition in every respect, inside and out; for handguns, "New In Box."

"Excellent" – all original parts; over 80 percent original finish; sharp lettering, numerals, and design on metal and wood; unmarred wood; fine bore.

"Fine" – all original parts; over 30 percent original finish; sharp lettering, numerals, and design on metal and wood; minor marks in wood; fine bore.

"Very Good" – all original parts; none to 30 percent original finish; original metal surfaces smooth with all edges sharp; clear lettering, numerals, and design on metal legible; wood refinished, scratched, bruised or minor cracks repaired; in good working order.

"Fair" – some major parts replaced; minor replacement parts may be required; metal rusted, may be lightly pitted all over, vigorously cleaned or reblued; rounded edges of metal and wood; principal lettering, numerals, and design on metal partly obliterated; wood scratched, bruised, cracked or repaired where broken; in fair working order or can easily be repaired and placed in working order.

"Poor" – major and minor parts replaced; replacement parts required and extensive restoration needed; metal deeply pitted; principal lettering, numerals, and design obliterated; wood badly scratched, bruised, cracked or broken; mechanically inoperative; generally undesirable as a collector's item.

---

generally of two kinds: smaller, more localized shows concentrating on modern or recent used firearms such as are sold in local gun shops; and larger shows in or near major cities, limited primarily to antique arms or those made before 1900. The latter can run to 500 to 1,000 tables or more, rented by both collectors and dealers, and devoted partly to displays of fine and historic arms not for sale. Entry may be open to the public for a nominal charge of $5 to $10, and such shows draw thousands of participants. Much of the buying and selling is done among the table holders, but members of the public are invited to bring in items to sell, as well as to buy. Again, schedules of the major shows are shown in the magazines listed in the bibliography. Anti-gun activists push for legislation to close the "gunshow loophole," claiming that many firearms are bought illegally at these shows; but there is no evidence of this; existing controls such as the Federal background check still apply, and the actual legislation which the anti-gunners support would take steps like imposing a three-day waiting period, which would close gun shows altogether.

Above: Rare, historic and deluxe Smith & Wesson Frontier revolver embellished by Tiffany & Co. as exhibited at the Chicago World's Fair of 1893 and subsequently presented to Anglophile and champion shot, Walter Winans.
(Courtesy Greg Martin Auctions.)

Prices of antique firearms have risen sometimes dramatically, like other collectibles; those specimens regarded as in higher range of fine and rare examples (including highly decorated specimens and those associated with prominent historic figures) have had substantial investment value. There is some faking, and other shady practices have been known at this level, so collectors need to be careful. Basically, the collector's real satisfaction comes from acquiring specimens he or she admires and which fit into a particular pattern of interest. At the same time, however, there is an occasional opportunity to make a good buy which will appreciate substantially in value; the writer admits to having told his wife on occasion that when he buys a gun, he is investing rather than spending!

The accompanying table was made in order to test the opinion sometimes heard that Colts are a better investment than Smith & Wessons. The estimates of value shown are from *Flayderman's Guide to Antique American Firearms* which tends to be followed quite closely in the prices offered by dealers and at gun shows. The conclusion, looking down

the list, is that the rate of increase has been quite consistent between Smith & Wessons and Colts. As expected, the table shows a higher rate of increase for specimens in the Fine to Excellent range of condition. In general, values approximately doubled in the 14 years from 1987 to 2001. This is the equivalent of a 7 percent per year return on money invested at the beginning of this period with compound interest, not a particularly good return if one is a speculator but a relatively safe investment in that gun values have never shown a year to year decline.

It should be noted that *Flayderman's Guide* covers only approximately up to the year 1900; the Supica and Nahas *Standard Catalog of Smith & Wesson* authoritatively covers all S&W issues since that time, including estimates of value. Supica and Nahas also report auction experience with some earlier models, such as a Schofield revolver in excellent condition which was sold at auction for $54,625 in 1999.

The finest museum collection of Smith & Wesson arms originated with the company itself, which kept or acquired many of its finest models and recently turned over the ownership of the collection to the Connecticut Valley Historical Museum in Springfield, Massachusetts, the company's home city. Most of the collection, some 1,700 arms, is in storage (in the original boxes) at the museum, but some are in display cases at the entrance to the company's office headquarters, and a fascinating group of experimental models is on display at the nearby Smith & Wesson retail store. The Smith & Wesson Collectors' Association has made a donation of $100,000 for the preservation, photography, and cataloguing of this collection plus its accompanying historical documents.

Museums in the East which exhibit Smith & Wessons include the National Firearms Museum of the National Rifle Association in Fairfax, Virginia, close to Washington, D.C.; the Smithsonian Institution in D.C.; the Metropolitan Museum of Art in New York, with its fine Tiffany-decorated collection; and the U.S. Military Academy Museum at West Point. The original Hunt-Jennings rifle and examples of the Smith & Wesson and Volcanic lever action pistols may be seen at the American Precision Museum in the original Robbins and Lawrence factory in Windsor, Vermont. Smith & Wesson Models 1 and 2 may be seen at Civil War museums such as at Gettysburg, Pennsylvania. In the West, the Smith & Wessons used on the frontier are featured in such museums as the Buffalo Bill Historical Center in Cody, Wyoming; the National Cowboy Hall of Fame and Western Heritage Center in Oklahoma City, Oklahoma; and the Gene Autry Museum of Western Heritage in Los Angeles, California. Smith & Wessons may not be as prominent in these collections as Colts and Winchesters, but the collector has the opportunity to see and identify models which may not be as widely known. There follows a visual review of highly collectible Smith & Wesson firearms from various periods, as well as some that are already in fine collections.

Comparison of values (in $US) between Smith & Wesson and Colt antique handguns, from *Flayderman's Guide to Antique American Firearms*, 4th and 8th editions

	Good	Very Good	Fine	Excellent
Smith & Wesson				
No.1 Second Issue .22, Standard early				
1987	110		200	
2001	175		425	
No. 2 Army, Standard, 3 pin, .32				
1987		275		625
2001		575		1750
First Model American .44, Standard				
1987	600		2000	
2001	1100		3750	
Schofield Military .45, early				
1987		1150		2500
2001		3300		8500
Colt				
1849 Pocket, .31, Standard				
1987	275		650	
2001	475		1100	
1851 Navy, .36, Third Model				
1987	425		1750	
2001	800		3850	
1860 Army, .44, Standard				
1987	425		2500	
2001	850		6000	
Single Action Army Peacemaker .45, Standard				
1987	575		1200	3750
2001	1200		4250	8500

U. S. GRANT 3RD
MAJOR GENERAL, U.S.A. RET'D
COLLEGE HILL
CLINTON, NEW YORK

7 April 1964.

My dear John,

I am glad to be able to certify for you that the 32 caliber, gold inlaid rim fire revolver you was your great Grandfather - I should have said your great, great Granfather Grant's and has been passed on to me through my Father, in whose possession was a cherished souvenir when he died in 1912. It can be identified by its serial number 41993.

I have no inside information as to any anecdotes connected with it, but feel sure he never killed any person or animal with it. Manifestly it must have been a present to him, probably from the manufacturer. You may be able to get further information about it from the Smith and Wweson firm.

In any case I am gld you have it, as I am sure you will prize it and take good care of it.

With love and best wishes for you and your parents and sisters,

Affectionately your Grandfather

Ulysses S. Grant 3rd

Left and below: Tremendous value, commercial and sentimental, may be added to a collector's piece if provenance is available, such as was the case with this Smith & Wesson 1¹/₂ New Issue revolver (see letter). The firearm was gold inlaid, engraved and with carved pearl grips by Gustave Young. It was a presentation by the factory to President Ulysses S. Grant. (Courtesy Greg Martin Auctions.)

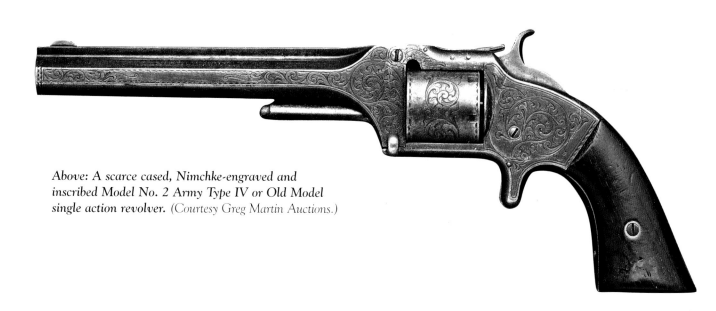

Above: A scarce cased, Nimchke-engraved and inscribed Model No. 2 Army Type IV or Old Model single action revolver. (Courtesy Greg Martin Auctions.)

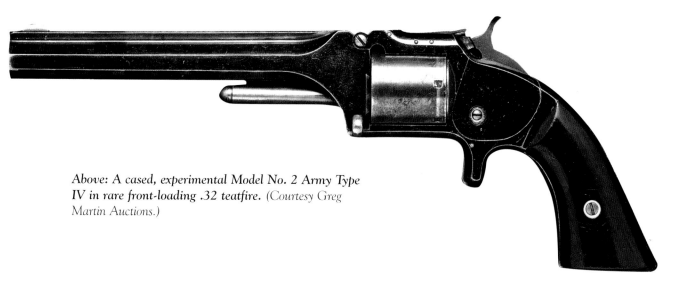

Above: A cased, experimental Model No. 2 Army Type IV in rare front-loading .32 teatfire. (Courtesy Greg Martin Auctions.)

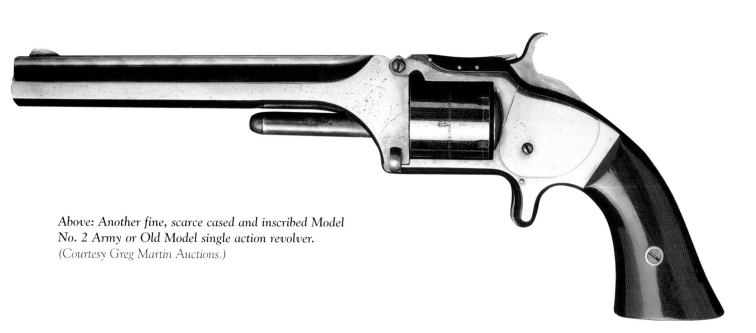

Above: Another fine, scarce cased and inscribed Model No. 2 Army or Old Model single action revolver. (Courtesy Greg Martin Auctions.)

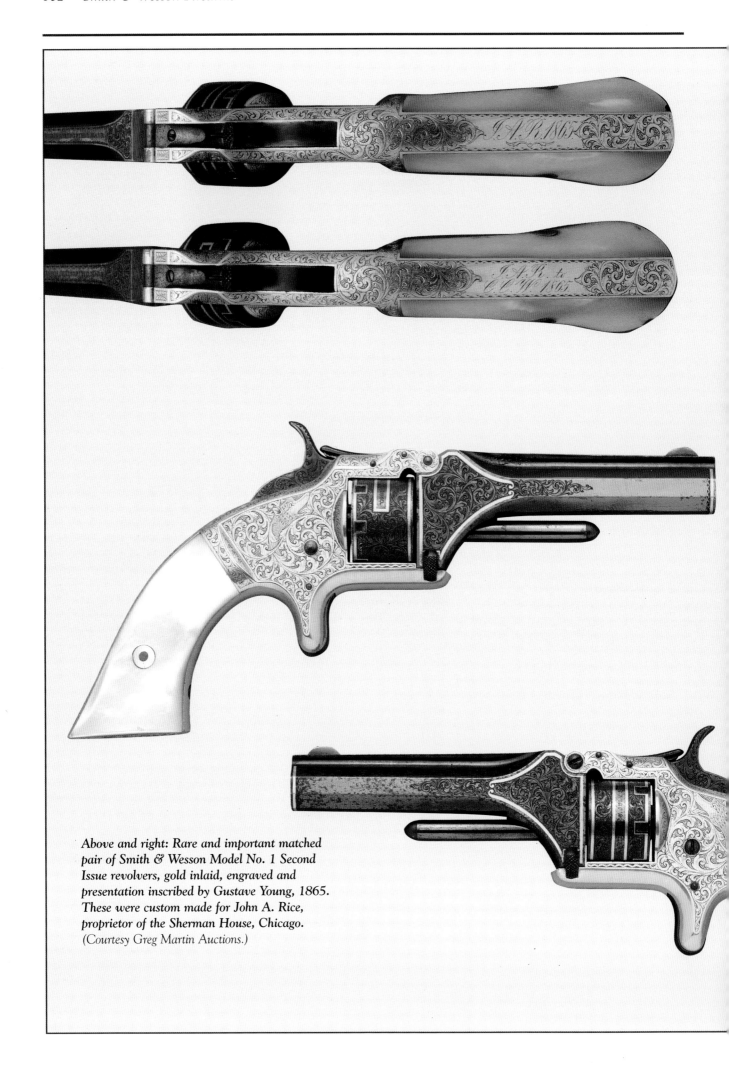

Above and right: *Rare and important matched pair of Smith & Wesson Model No. 1 Second Issue revolvers, gold inlaid, engraved and presentation inscribed by Gustave Young, 1865. These were custom made for John A. Rice, proprietor of the Sherman House, Chicago.* (Courtesy Greg Martin Auctions.)

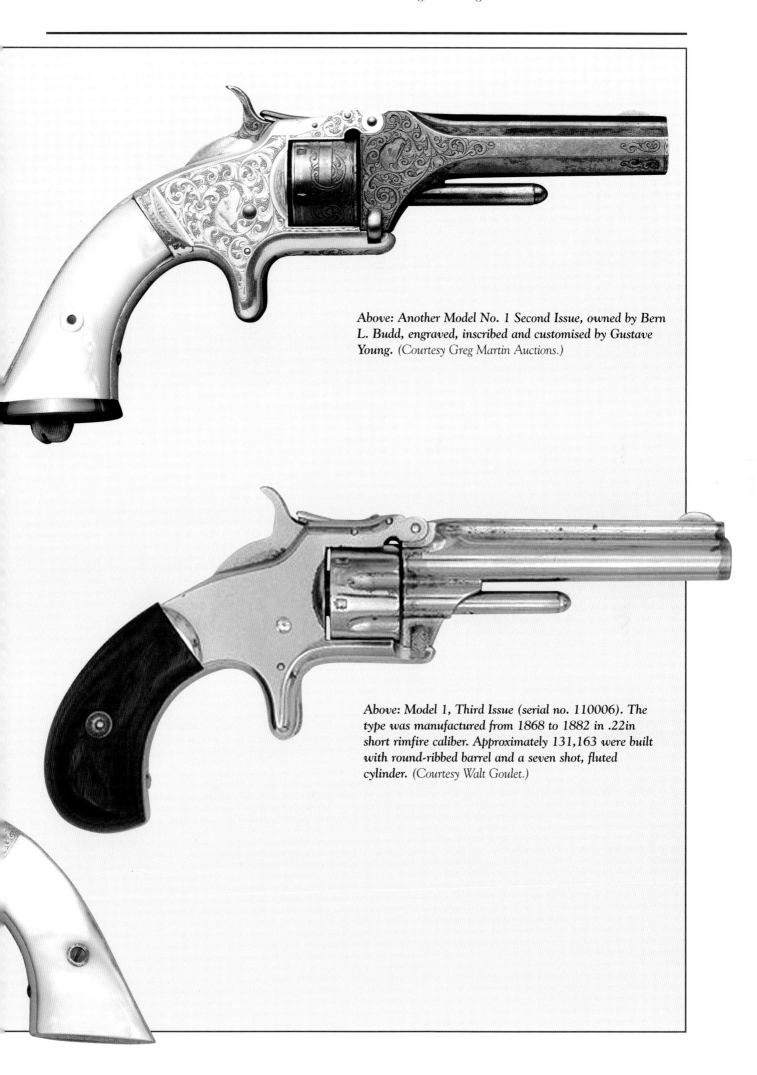

Above: Another Model No. 1 Second Issue, owned by Bern L. Budd, engraved, inscribed and customised by Gustave Young. (Courtesy Greg Martin Auctions.)

Above: Model 1, Third Issue (serial no. 110006). The type was manufactured from 1868 to 1882 in .22in short rimfire caliber. Approximately 131,163 were built with round-ribbed barrel and a seven shot, fluted cylinder. (Courtesy Walt Goulet.)

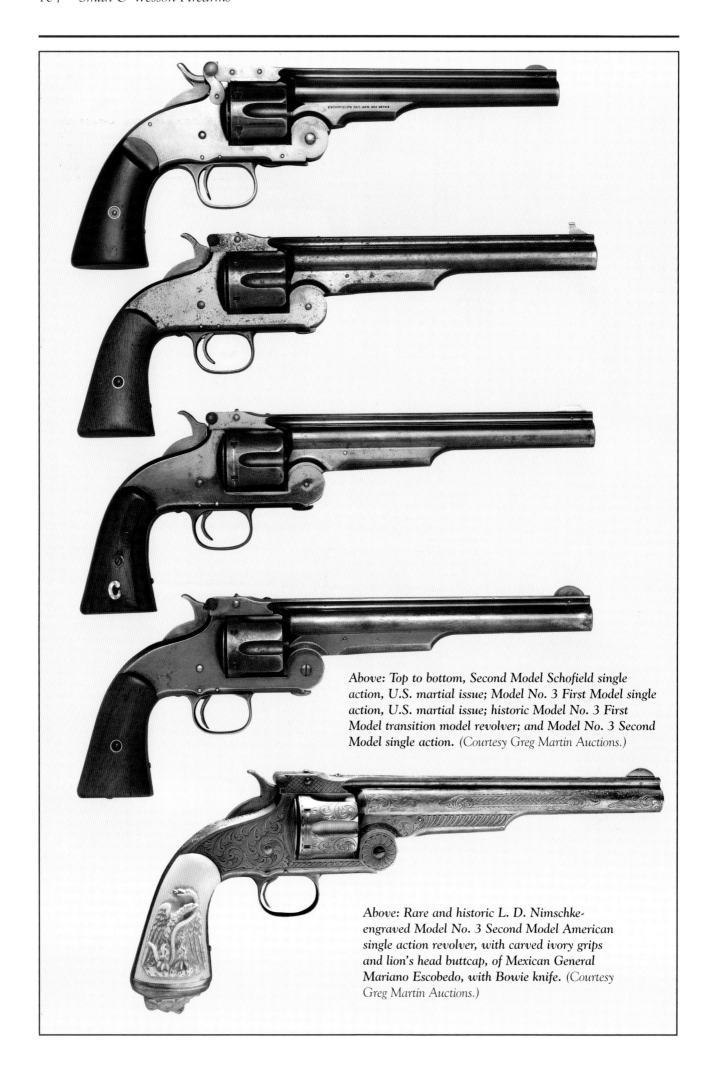

Above: Top to bottom, Second Model Schofield single action, U.S. martial issue; Model No. 3 First Model single action, U.S. martial issue; historic Model No. 3 First Model transition model revolver; and Model No. 3 Second Model single action. *(Courtesy Greg Martin Auctions.)*

Above: Rare and historic L. D. Nimschke-engraved Model No. 3 Second Model American single action revolver, with carved ivory grips and lion's head buttcap, of Mexican General Mariano Escobedo, with Bowie knife. *(Courtesy Greg Martin Auctions.)*

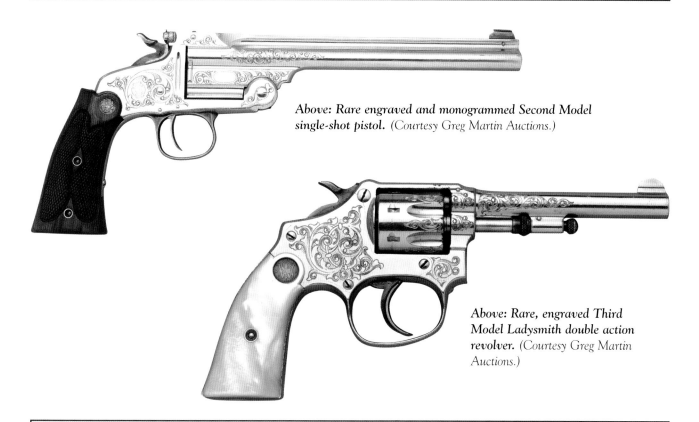

Above: Rare engraved and monogrammed Second Model single-shot pistol. (Courtesy Greg Martin Auctions.)

Above: Rare, engraved Third Model Ladysmith double action revolver. (Courtesy Greg Martin Auctions.)

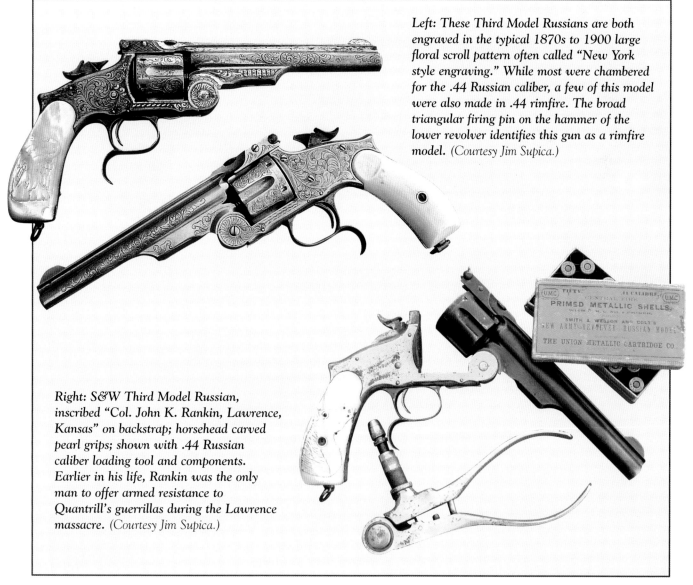

Left: These Third Model Russians are both engraved in the typical 1870s to 1900 large floral scroll pattern often called "New York style engraving." While most were chambered for the .44 Russian caliber, a few of this model were also made in .44 rimfire. The broad triangular firing pin on the hammer of the lower revolver identifies this gun as a rimfire model. (Courtesy Jim Supica.)

Right: S&W Third Model Russian, inscribed "Col. John K. Rankin, Lawrence, Kansas" on backstrap; horsehead carved pearl grips; shown with .44 Russian caliber loading tool and components. Earlier in his life, Rankin was the only man to offer armed resistance to Quantrill's guerrillas during the Lawrence massacre. (Courtesy Jim Supica.)

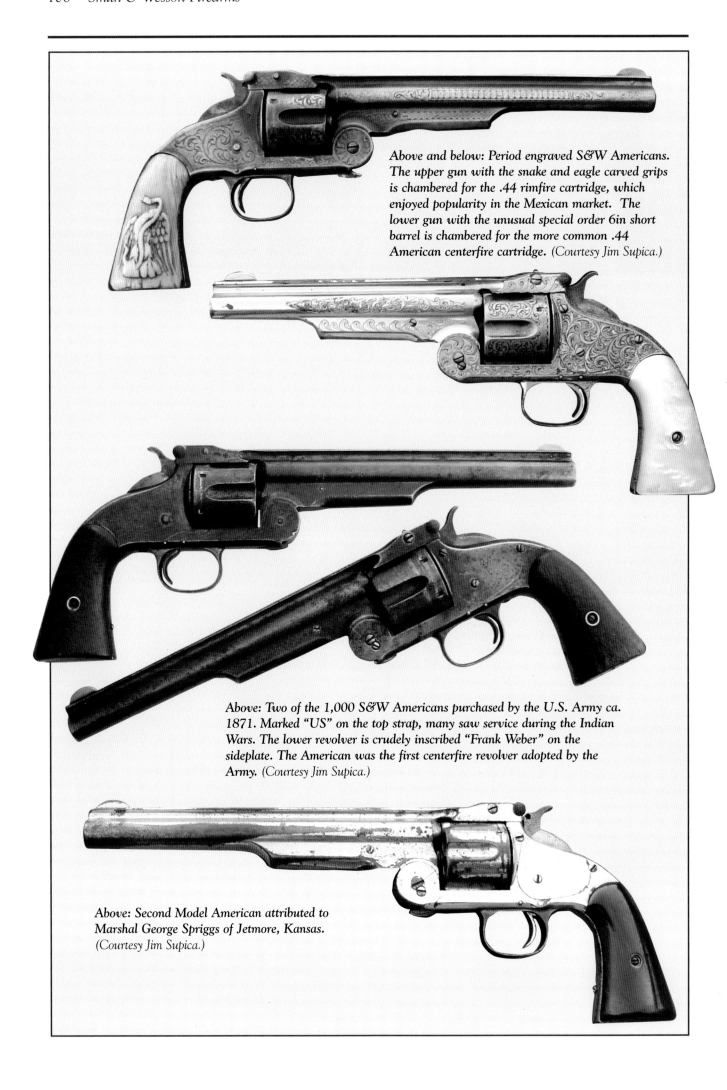

Above and below: Period engraved S&W Americans. The upper gun with the snake and eagle carved grips is chambered for the .44 rimfire cartridge, which enjoyed popularity in the Mexican market. The lower gun with the unusual special order 6in short barrel is chambered for the more common .44 American centerfire cartridge. (Courtesy Jim Supica.)

Above: Two of the 1,000 S&W Americans purchased by the U.S. Army ca. 1871. Marked "US" on the top strap, many saw service during the Indian Wars. The lower revolver is crudely inscribed "Frank Weber" on the sideplate. The American was the first centerfire revolver adopted by the Army. (Courtesy Jim Supica.)

Above: Second Model American attributed to Marshal George Spriggs of Jetmore, Kansas. (Courtesy Jim Supica.)

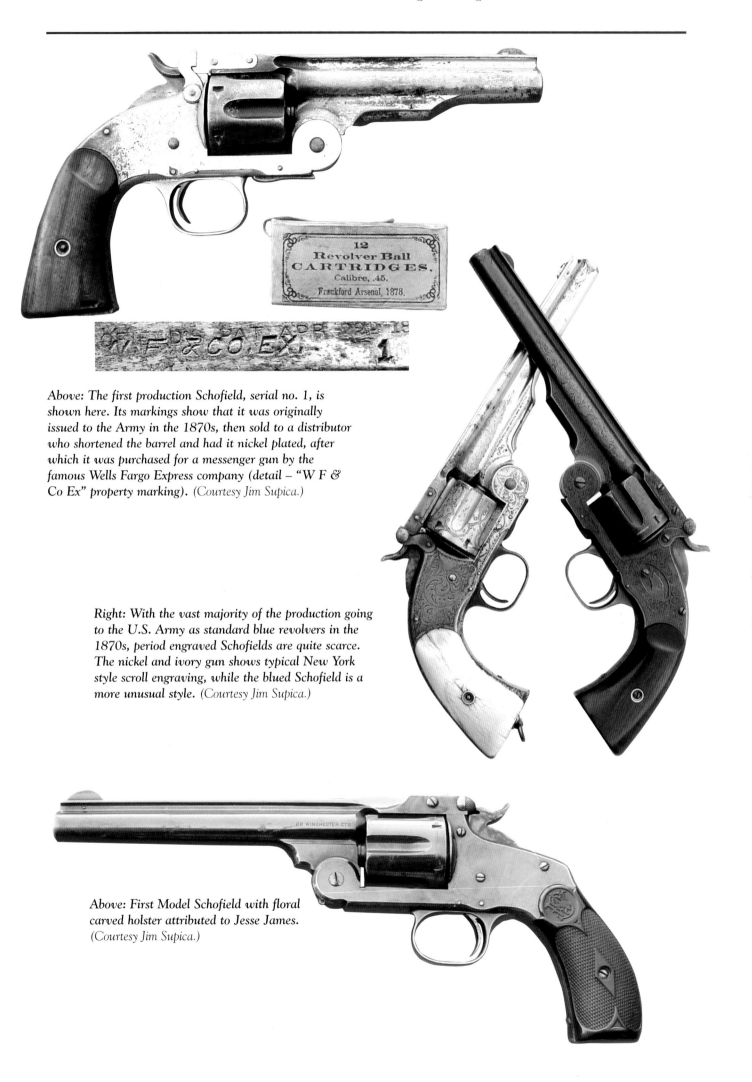

Above: The first production Schofield, serial no. 1, is shown here. Its markings show that it was originally issued to the Army in the 1870s, then sold to a distributor who shortened the barrel and had it nickel plated, after which it was purchased for a messenger gun by the famous Wells Fargo Express company (detail – "W F & Co Ex" property marking). *(Courtesy Jim Supica.)*

Right: With the vast majority of the production going to the U.S. Army as standard blue revolvers in the 1870s, period engraved Schofields are quite scarce. The nickel and ivory gun shows typical New York style scroll engraving, while the blued Schofield is a more unusual style. *(Courtesy Jim Supica.)*

Above: First Model Schofield with floral carved holster attributed to Jesse James. *(Courtesy Jim Supica.)*

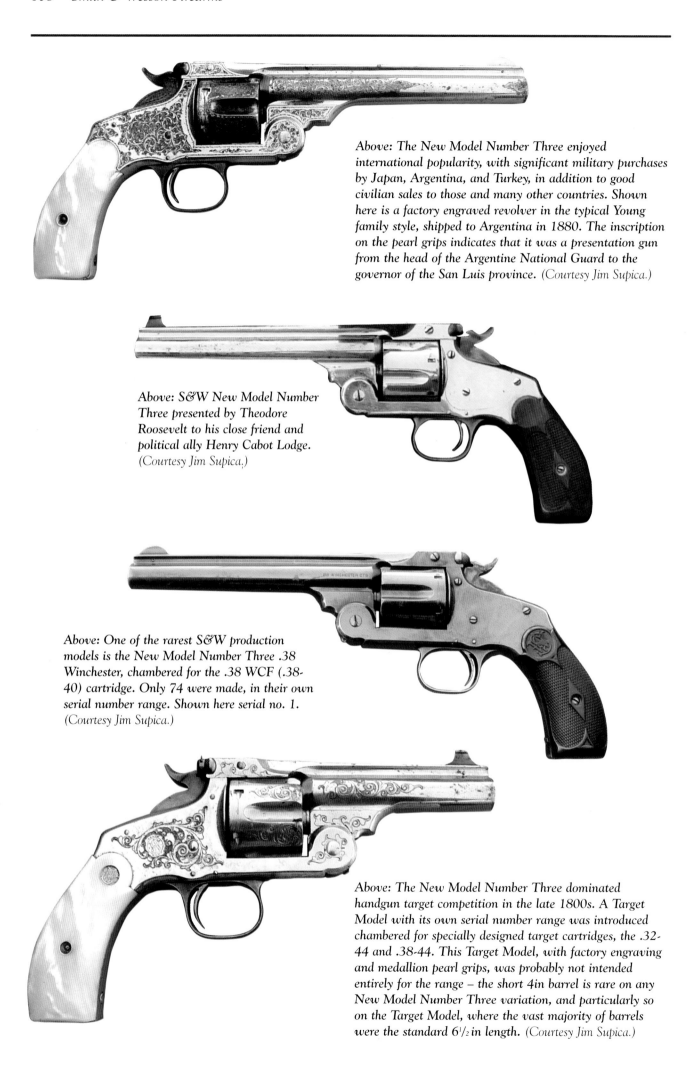

Above: The New Model Number Three enjoyed international popularity, with significant military purchases by Japan, Argentina, and Turkey, in addition to good civilian sales to those and many other countries. Shown here is a factory engraved revolver in the typical Young family style, shipped to Argentina in 1880. The inscription on the pearl grips indicates that it was a presentation gun from the head of the Argentine National Guard to the governor of the San Luis province. (Courtesy Jim Supica.)

Above: S&W New Model Number Three presented by Theodore Roosevelt to his close friend and political ally Henry Cabot Lodge. (Courtesy Jim Supica.)

Above: One of the rarest S&W production models is the New Model Number Three .38 Winchester, chambered for the .38 WCF (.38-40) cartridge. Only 74 were made, in their own serial number range. Shown here serial no. 1. (Courtesy Jim Supica.)

Above: The New Model Number Three dominated handgun target competition in the late 1800s. A Target Model with its own serial number range was introduced chambered for specially designed target cartridges, the .32-44 and .38-44. This Target Model, with factory engraving and medallion pearl grips, was probably not intended entirely for the range – the short 4in barrel is rare on any New Model Number Three variation, and particularly so on the Target Model, where the vast majority of barrels were the standard 6¹/₂ in length. (Courtesy Jim Supica.)

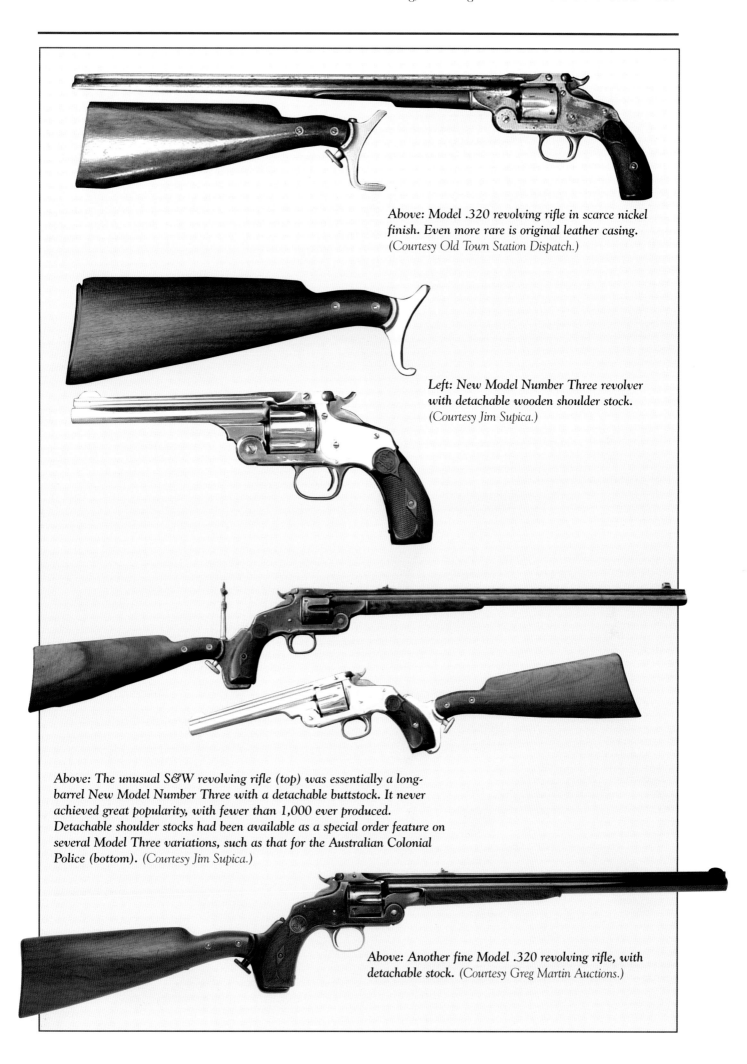

Above: Model .320 revolving rifle in scarce nickel finish. Even more rare is original leather casing. (Courtesy Old Town Station Dispatch.)

Left: New Model Number Three revolver with detachable wooden shoulder stock. (Courtesy Jim Supica.)

Above: The unusual S&W revolving rifle (top) was essentially a long-barrel New Model Number Three with a detachable buttstock. It never achieved great popularity, with fewer than 1,000 ever produced. Detachable shoulder stocks had been available as a special order feature on several Model Three variations, such as that for the Australian Colonial Police (bottom). (Courtesy Jim Supica.)

Above: Another fine Model .320 revolving rifle, with detachable stock. (Courtesy Greg Martin Auctions.)

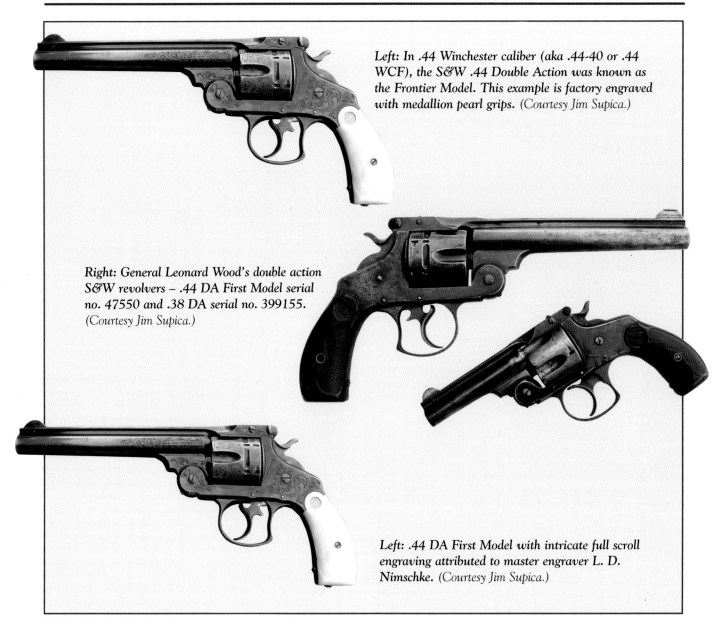

Left: In .44 Winchester caliber (aka .44-40 or .44 WCF), the S&W .44 Double Action was known as the Frontier Model. This example is factory engraved with medallion pearl grips. (Courtesy Jim Supica.)

Right: General Leonard Wood's double action S&W revolvers – .44 DA First Model serial no. 47550 and .38 DA serial no. 399155. (Courtesy Jim Supica.)

Left: .44 DA First Model with intricate full scroll engraving attributed to master engraver L. D. Nimschke. (Courtesy Jim Supica.)

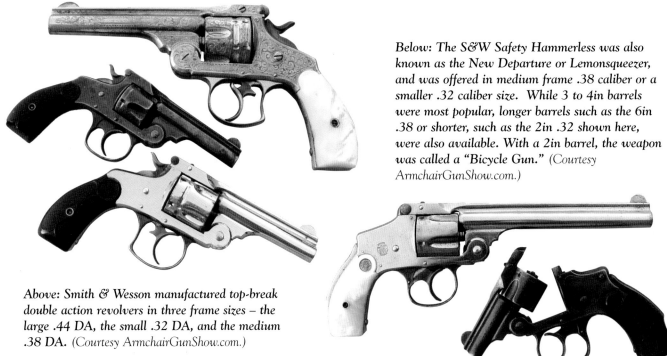

Below: The S&W Safety Hammerless was also known as the New Departure or Lemonsqueezer, and was offered in medium frame .38 caliber or a smaller .32 caliber size. While 3 to 4in barrels were most popular, longer barrels such as the 6in .38 or shorter, such as the 2in .32 shown here, were also available. With a 2in barrel, the weapon was called a "Bicycle Gun." (Courtesy ArmchairGunShow.com.)

Above: Smith & Wesson manufactured top-break double action revolvers in three frame sizes – the large .44 DA, the small .32 DA, and the medium .38 DA. (Courtesy ArmchairGunShow.com.)

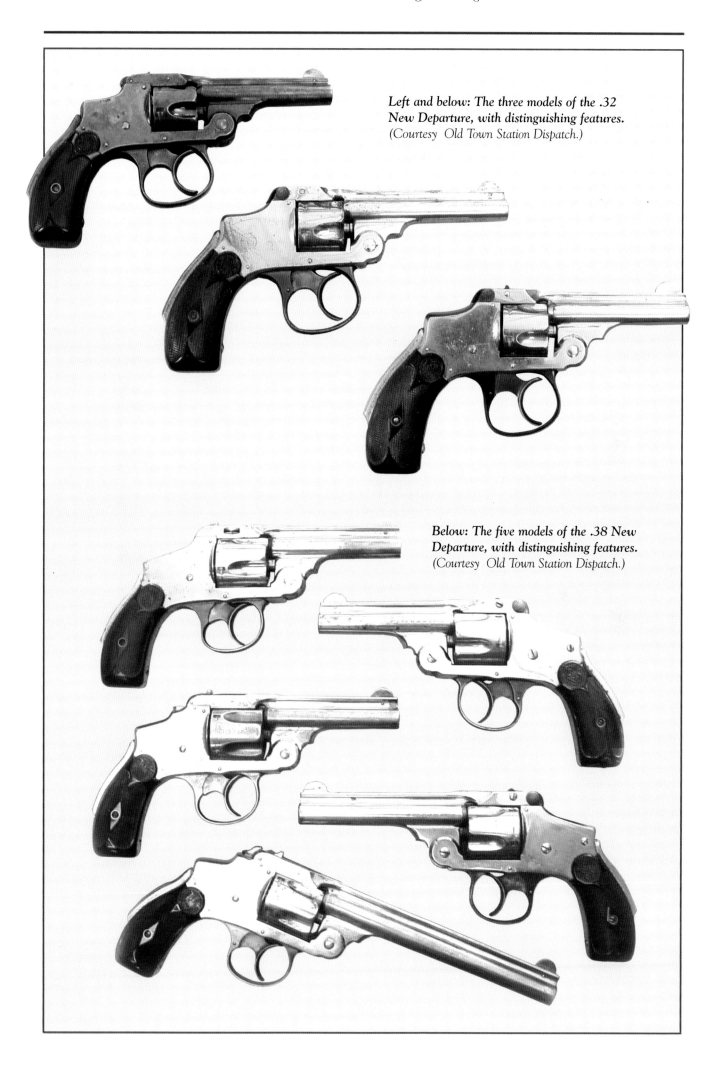

Left and below: The three models of the .32 New Departure, with distinguishing features. (Courtesy Old Town Station Dispatch.)

Below: The five models of the .38 New Departure, with distinguishing features. (Courtesy Old Town Station Dispatch.)

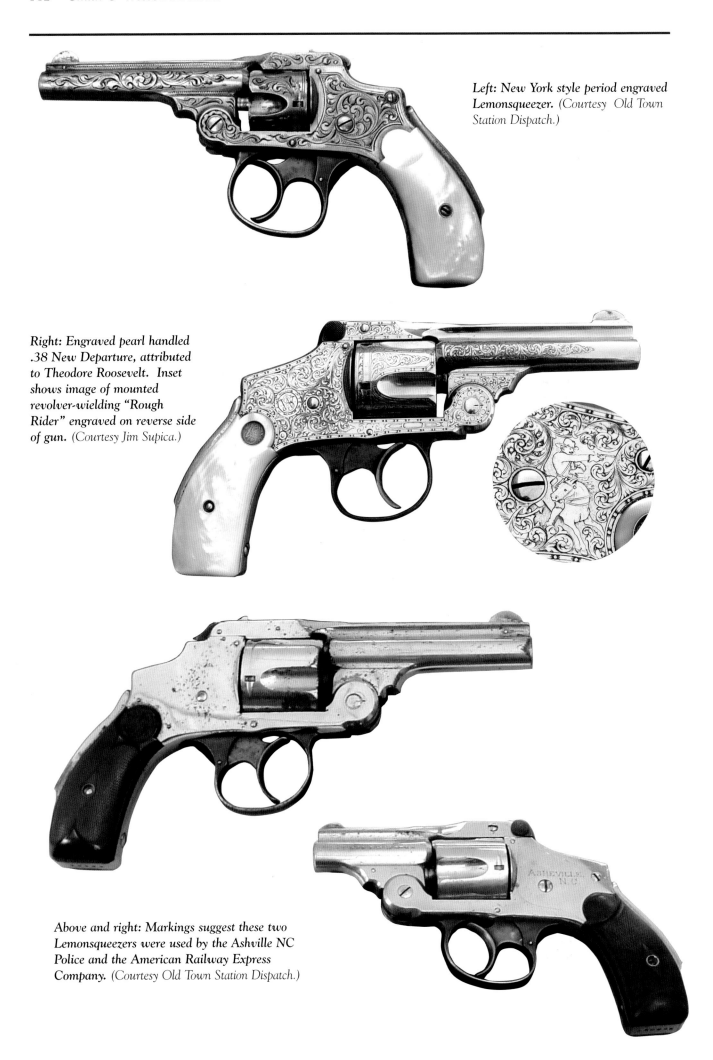

Left: New York style period engraved Lemonsqueezer. (Courtesy Old Town Station Dispatch.)

Right: Engraved pearl handled .38 New Departure, attributed to Theodore Roosevelt. Inset shows image of mounted revolver-wielding "Rough Rider" engraved on reverse side of gun. (Courtesy Jim Supica.)

Above and right: Markings suggest these two Lemonsqueezers were used by the Ashville NC Police and the American Railway Express Company. (Courtesy Old Town Station Dispatch.)

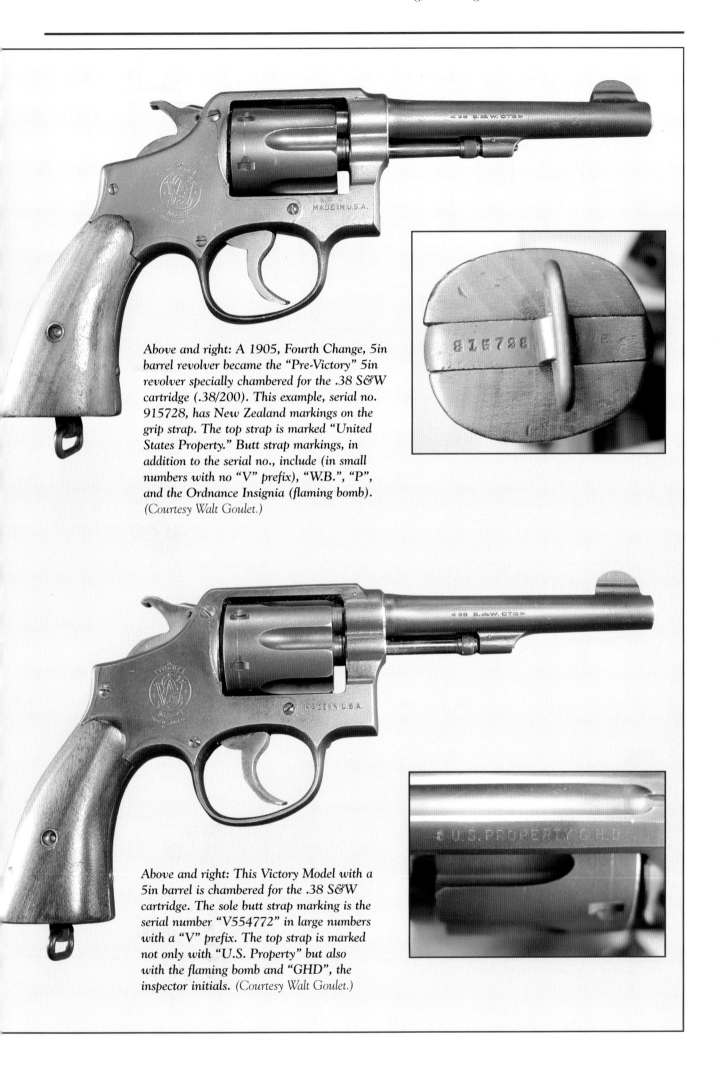

Above and right: A 1905, Fourth Change, 5in barrel revolver became the "Pre-Victory" 5in revolver specially chambered for the .38 S&W cartridge (.38/200). This example, serial no. 915728, has New Zealand markings on the grip strap. The top strap is marked "United States Property." Butt strap markings, in addition to the serial no., include (in small numbers with no "V" prefix), "W.B.", "P", and the Ordnance Insignia (flaming bomb). (Courtesy Walt Goulet.)

Above and right: This Victory Model with a 5in barrel is chambered for the .38 S&W cartridge. The sole butt strap marking is the serial number "V554772" in large numbers with a "V" prefix. The top strap is marked not only with "U.S. Property" but also with the flaming bomb and "GHD", the inspector initials. (Courtesy Walt Goulet.)

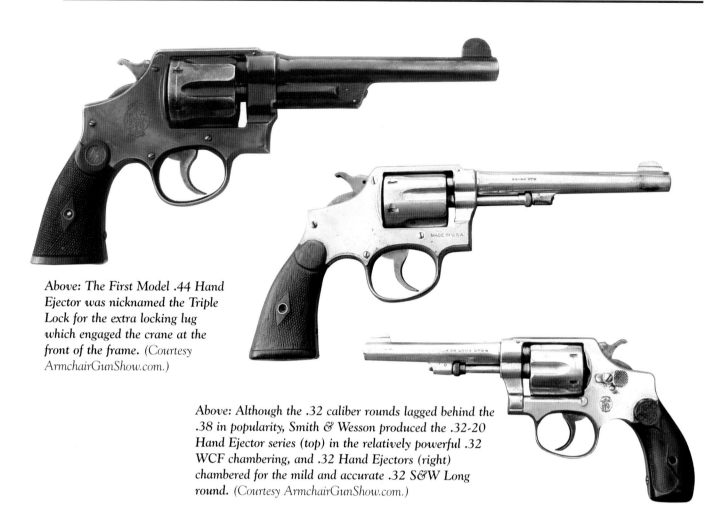

Above: The First Model .44 Hand Ejector was nicknamed the Triple Lock for the extra locking lug which engaged the crane at the front of the frame. (Courtesy ArmchairGunShow.com.)

Above: Although the .32 caliber rounds lagged behind the .38 in popularity, Smith & Wesson produced the .32-20 Hand Ejector series (top) in the relatively powerful .32 WCF chambering, and .32 Hand Ejectors (right) chambered for the mild and accurate .32 S&W Long round. (Courtesy ArmchairGunShow.com.)

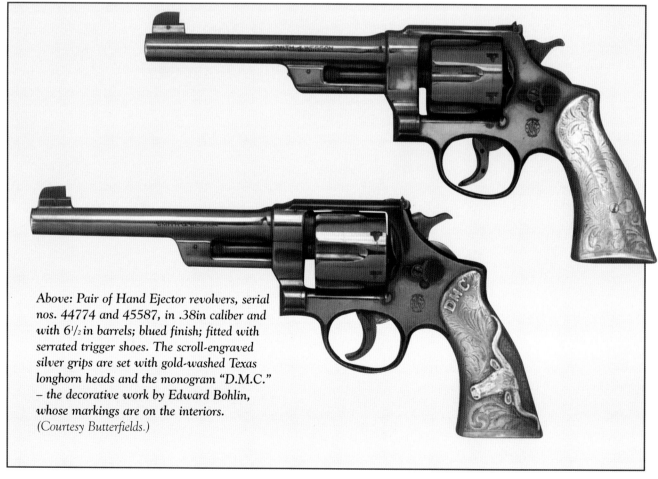

Above: Pair of Hand Ejector revolvers, serial nos. 44774 and 45587, in .38in caliber and with 6¹/₂ in barrels; blued finish; fitted with serrated trigger shoes. The scroll-engraved silver grips are set with gold-washed Texas longhorn heads and the monogram "D.M.C." – the decorative work by Edward Bohlin, whose markings are on the interiors. (Courtesy Butterfields.)

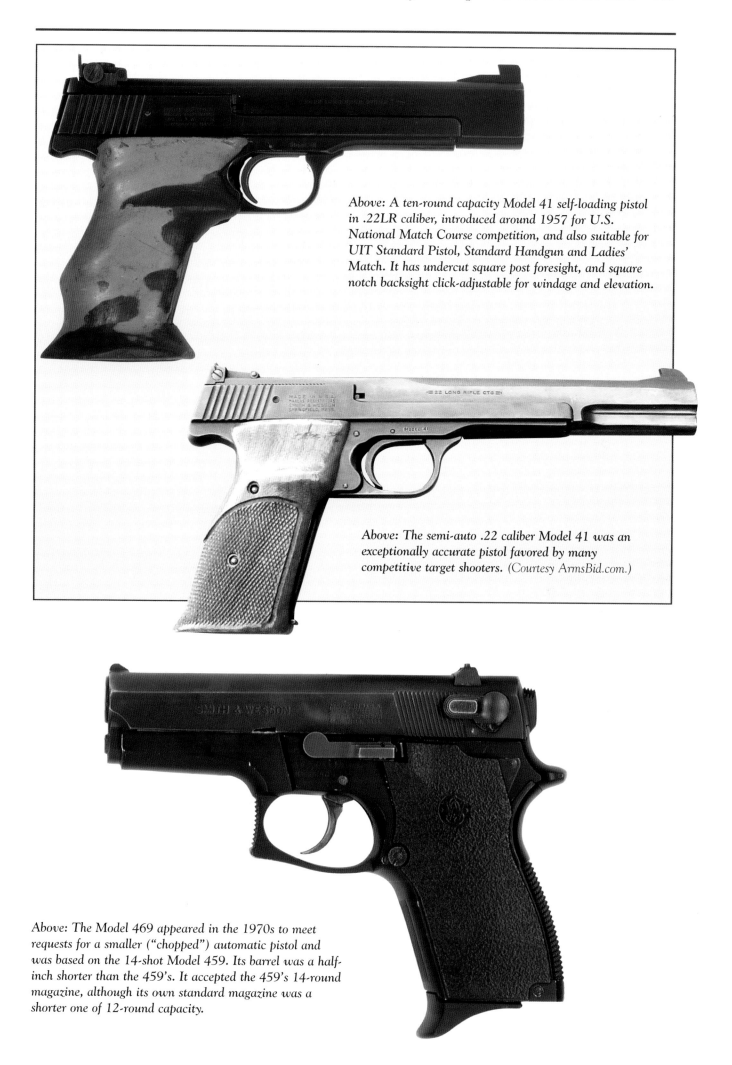

Above: A ten-round capacity Model 41 self-loading pistol in .22LR caliber, introduced around 1957 for U.S. National Match Course competition, and also suitable for UIT Standard Pistol, Standard Handgun and Ladies' Match. It has undercut square post foresight, and square notch backsight click-adjustable for windage and elevation.

Above: The semi-auto .22 caliber Model 41 was an exceptionally accurate pistol favored by many competitive target shooters. *(Courtesy ArmsBid.com.)*

Above: The Model 469 appeared in the 1970s to meet requests for a smaller ("chopped") automatic pistol and was based on the 14-shot Model 459. Its barrel was a half-inch shorter than the 459's. It accepted the 459's 14-round magazine, although its own standard magazine was a shorter one of 12-round capacity.

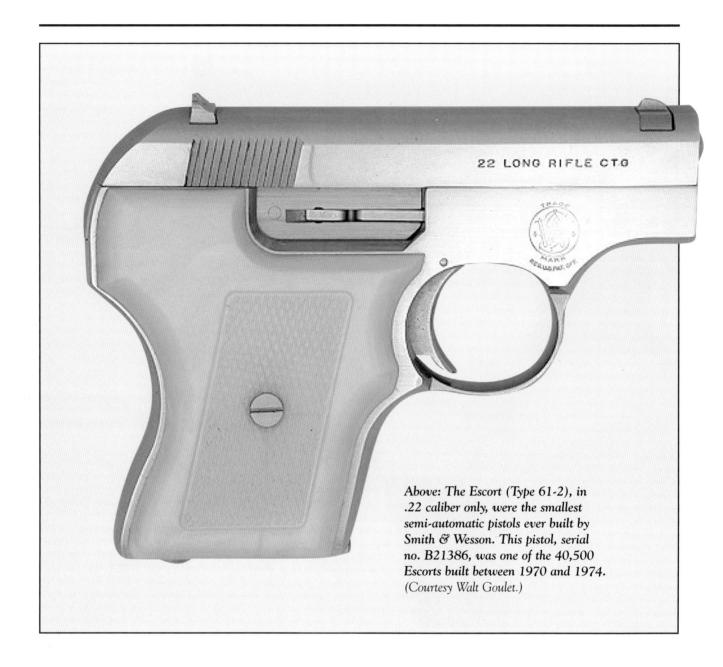

Above: The Escort (Type 61-2), in
.22 caliber only, were the smallest
semi-automatic pistols ever built by
Smith & Wesson. This pistol, serial
no. B21386, was one of the 40,500
Escorts built between 1970 and 1974.
(Courtesy Walt Goulet.)

Above: Model 586 (blued steel) and, as here, Model
686 (stainless steel) were 0.357 caliber, 6in-barrel
revolvers introduced in 1981 in direct competition
with Colt's Python.

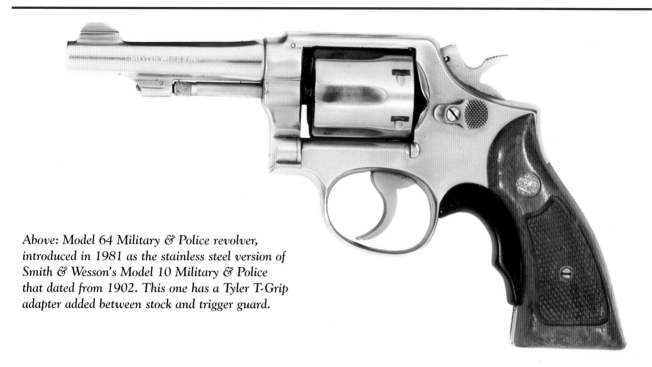

Above: Model 64 Military & Police revolver, introduced in 1981 as the stainless steel version of Smith & Wesson's Model 10 Military & Police that dated from 1902. This one has a Tyler T-Grip adapter added between stock and trigger guard.

Above: The .38in caliber Model 14 K38 Masterpiece (top) was one of the most successful and popular target revolvers ever made. Lower photo shows the 14-4 K38 model.

Above: About 1990, Smith & Wesson and distributor Ellett Brothers co-operated to produce a limited production series of "Twelve Revolvers," one to be shipped each month for a year. Each revolver was a popular model in a unique configuration, laser-etched with a scene based on the famous S&W advertising photos from the early 1900s. Each model type is identified, with its limited production name, on this and the following two pages, beginning with: "The Hostiles," a Model 29 blue .44 Magnum N-frame, 8³/₈in barrel, target features. *(Photos of all "Twelve Revolvers" series courtesy Jim Supica.)*

Above: "With the Wolfhounds," Model 686 stainless steel Distinguished Combat Magnum .357 Magnum L-frame, 6in full lug barrel.

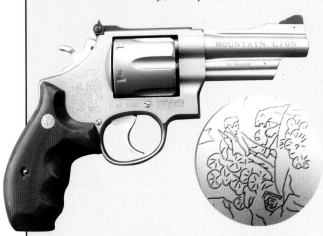

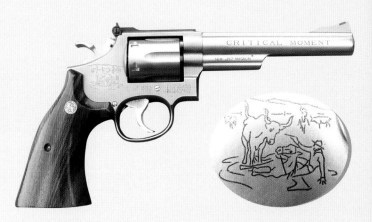

Above: "Mountain Lion," Model 629 stainless steel .44 Magnum N-frame in Mountain Revolver configuration consisting of short light 4in barrel, chambered cylinder, smooth combat trigger and finger-groove smooth combat grips.

Above "Critical Moment," Model 66 stainless steel Combat Magnum K-frame .357 Magnum, 6in barrel, target features.

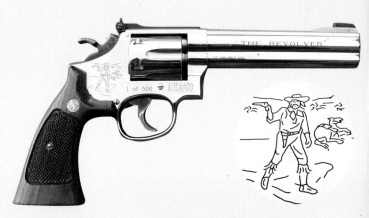

Above: "Last Cartridge," Model 57 blue .41 Magnum Target N-frame, 6in barrel.

Above: "The Revolver," Model 17 nickel K-22 Masterpiece, .22 LR, 6in full-lug barrel, target features.

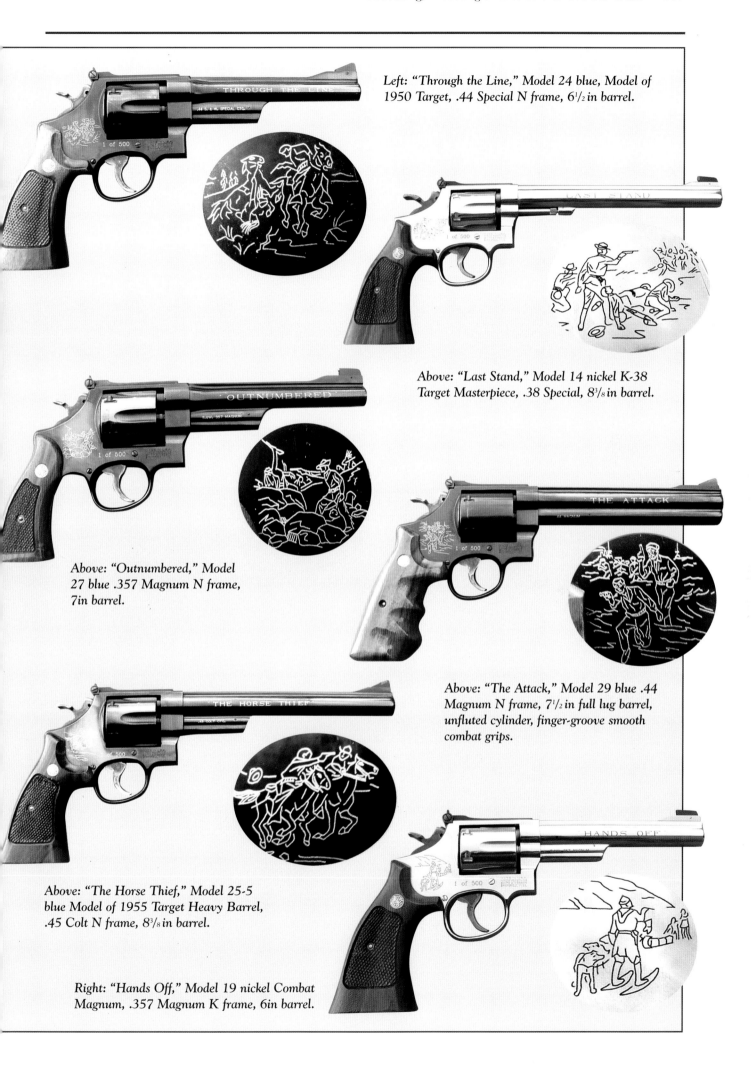

Left: "Through the Line," Model 24 blue, Model of 1950 Target, .44 Special N frame, 6½ in barrel.

Above: "Last Stand," Model 14 nickel K-38 Target Masterpiece, .38 Special, 8³/₈ in barrel.

Above: "Outnumbered," Model 27 blue .357 Magnum N frame, 7in barrel.

Above: "The Attack," Model 29 blue .44 Magnum N frame, 7½ in full lug barrel, unfluted cylinder, finger-groove smooth combat grips.

Above: "The Horse Thief," Model 25-5 blue Model of 1955 Target Heavy Barrel, .45 Colt N frame, 8³/₈ in barrel.

Right: "Hands Off," Model 19 nickel Combat Magnum, .357 Magnum K frame, 6in barrel.

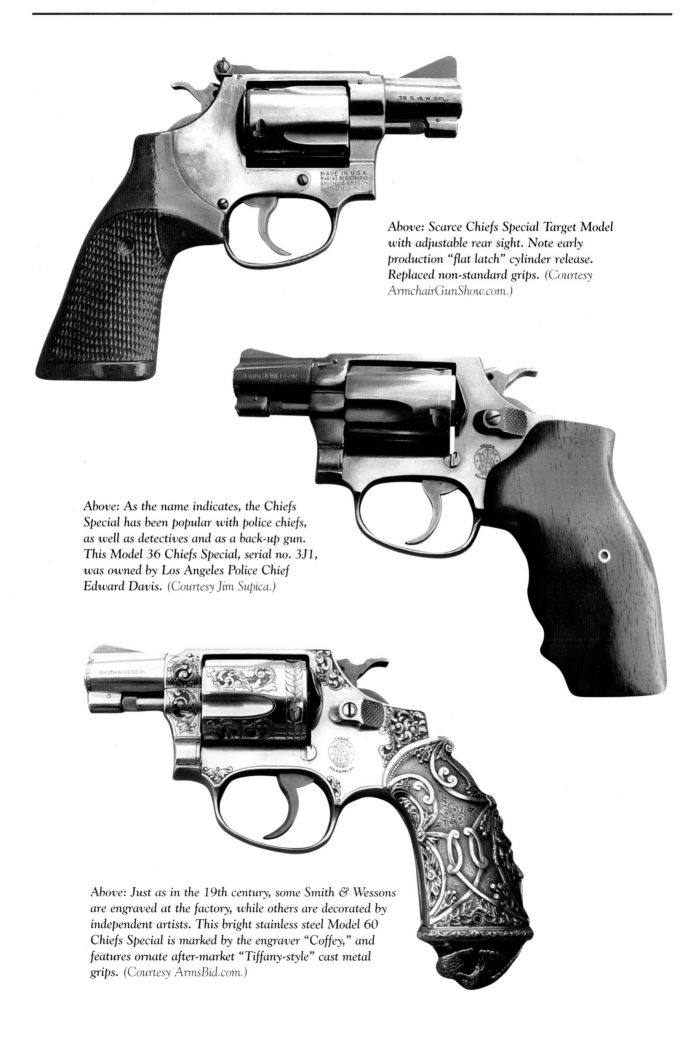

Above: Scarce Chiefs Special Target Model with adjustable rear sight. Note early production "flat latch" cylinder release. Replaced non-standard grips. (Courtesy ArmchairGunShow.com.)

Above: As the name indicates, the Chiefs Special has been popular with police chiefs, as well as detectives and as a back-up gun. This Model 36 Chiefs Special, serial no. 3J1, was owned by Los Angeles Police Chief Edward Davis. (Courtesy Jim Supica.)

Above: Just as in the 19th century, some Smith & Wessons are engraved at the factory, while others are decorated by independent artists. This bright stainless steel Model 60 Chiefs Special is marked by the engraver "Coffey," and features ornate after-market "Tiffany-style" cast metal grips. (Courtesy ArmsBid.com.)

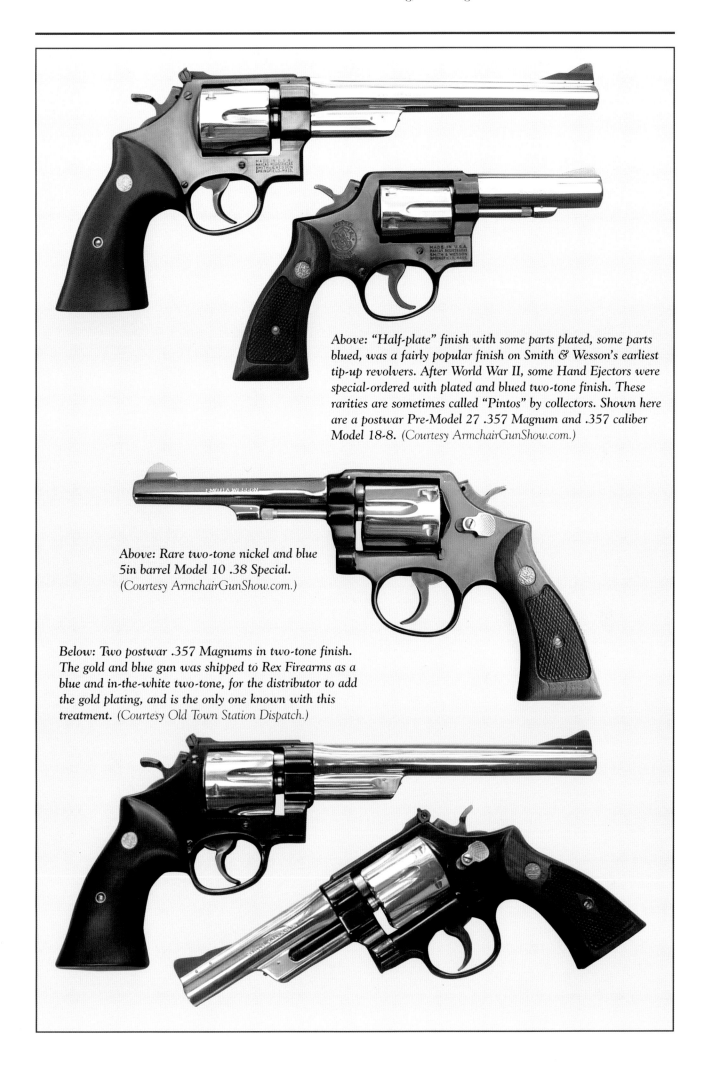

Above: "Half-plate" finish with some parts plated, some parts blued, was a fairly popular finish on Smith & Wesson's earliest tip-up revolvers. After World War II, some Hand Ejectors were special-ordered with plated and blued two-tone finish. These rarities are sometimes called "Pintos" by collectors. Shown here are a postwar Pre-Model 27 .357 Magnum and .357 caliber Model 18-8. (Courtesy ArmchairGunShow.com.)

Above: Rare two-tone nickel and blue 5in barrel Model 10 .38 Special. (Courtesy ArmchairGunShow.com.)

Below: Two postwar .357 Magnums in two-tone finish. The gold and blue gun was shipped to Rex Firearms as a blue and in-the-white two-tone, for the distributor to add the gold plating, and is the only one known with this treatment. (Courtesy Old Town Station Dispatch.)

FIRING THE GUNS

An advantage of collecting Smith & Wesson firearms is that even the oldest, if in good condition, can be fired with ammunition that is commercially available. However, in another sense this may be a disadvantage, in that the same handgun laws and restrictions may apply that have been adopted in some states for modern handguns.

All Smith & Wessons before the late 1890s used black powder cartridges, so care must be exercised in using the

Test Gun No.	Model	Powder charge	Bullet weight, grains	Muzzle velocity, feet per second	Muzzle energy, foot pounds	Hand rest target group, inches	Range, feet
1	Model 1 First Issue .22 Short, 1860-68	factory		786	38	4¹/₂	25
2	Model 2 Army .32, 1851-74	factory, (short)		850	128	3	25
3	Baby Russian .38 S&W, First Model Single Action 1866-1867	2¹/₂ grains	158	400	150	2	25
4	Double Action First Model .38 S&W, 1880	2¹/₂ grains	158	400	150	1¹/₂	25
5	U.S. Service Model 1917, .45 ACP	factory	230	780	356	1¹/₂	25
6	Model 10 Military & Police .38 Special 1940s	factory		672	200	1¹/₂	25
7	Model 41 .22 Long Rifle automatic, modern	factory		1030	95	3¹/₄	50
8	Model 340 AirLite Sc .357 Magnum, modern, 2in barrel	factory	110	1068	535	1¹/₂	25
9	Model 33 Regulation Police, .38 S&W, modern, 2in barrel	factory		685	150	3¹/₂	50
10	Model 36 Chiefs Special, .38 Special, modern	factory	132	672	200	3¹/₄	25
11	Model 1006 .40 S&W Automatic, modern	factory		980	382	3	50
12	Model 29-3 .44 Magnum, modern, 6in barrel, ported	factory	240	1350	971	2	50
13	Model 29-2 .44 Magnum, modern, 8 ³/₈in barrel, telescopic sight, not ported	factory	240	1350	971	2	50
14	Model 25-2 automatic with telescopic sight .45 ACP, modern	factory		780	356	2	75

more powerful smokeless powder. Modern manufacturers take this into account in the amount of smokeless powder that is used in current commercial ammunition, so this caution applies mainly to handloaders.

As an informal comparison of the performance of the major Smith & Wesson models, antique and modern, a test firing was conducted with friends and members of a collectors' association. The accompanying table shows the interesting results. All the guns fired, from the 1860 First Model .22 through the recent .44 Magnums, performed exactly as they should, with no misfires or even stray shots off the target paper. Smith & Wesson has always emphasized reliability and quality: our test firing showed they got it right!

An attempt was made to record the actual muzzle velocity of each of the handguns fired, by means of a Pro-Tach chronograph made by Competition Electronics, Inc. This is a plastic bar mounted on a tripod parallel to the direction of firing, and with cardboard frames on top 18 inches apart. The shooter fires through openings in the cardboard frames, and the chronograph senses the bullet's shadow and records the time taken to pass between the two frames. A number representing the speed and feet per second appears at the end of the bar facing the shooter (the device operates with a 9 volt battery). The only problem is when the bullet hits the end of the bar itself, which is what happened partway through our test firing!

Above: .22 Short Model 1 First Issue.

Above: Model 2 Army.

Above and right: Baby Russian (and detail showing recoil)

Above: Double Action First Model.

Above: Model 10 Military & Police.

Above: Model 41, .22in caliber, little recoil.

The bullet being used was only a .22 Short so the damage to the device was not extensive. The remaining speeds shown on the accompanying table are from a standard reference book, Frank Barnes' *Cartridges of the World*. Since primarily factory loads were used in the test firing, the data shown are reasonably reliable.

The short ranges used for some of the handguns, 25 feet, was chosen in order to make sure that the shots were on the target paper so that the grouping could be measured. In most instances, however, the standard pistol competition range of 25 yards or 75 feet could have been used just as well. A series of conclusions from this informal test is as follows:

The low power in foot pounds as limited accuracy of the First Model .22 is consistent with derogatory comments made by denizens of the Old West like Mark Twain, who spoke of it as Smith & Wesson's pitiful little seven-shooter with a ball like a homeopathic pill, and scoffed at its lack of accuracy. However, this is belied by the pistol's substantial sales in three models, from 1857 to 1881.

The modern Model 41 automatic with the .22in Long Rifle cartridge has more speed and power than the .22 Short, and its accuracy reflects its design as a target pistol. However, its power is still generally comparable to the .22 Short cartridge which was used by the first Smith & Wesson revolver, the Model 1, and illustrates the continuing popularity of the company's original pioneering effort. The .22 Short cartridge is still made for use in older handguns and rifles.

The Model 2 Army in .32in caliber, the only cartridge revolver in the Civil War, showed reasonable speed and accuracy, even with the .32 Short cartridge used; the pistol was actually designed to use the more powerful .32in Long cartridge. It is interesting to compare its power with the contemporary Colt percussion pistols, the 1849 Pocket Model in .31 caliber, the 1851 Navy in .36 caliber, and the 1860 Army in .44 caliber. The muzzle energies of the three are shown in the accompanying volume, *The History of Colt Firearms*, as 73, 157, and 336, respectively. The Smith & Wesson .32 is comparable in power to the Colt Navy, which was a particularly popular sidearm in the Civil War for soldiers not issued the Army model. If the Ordnance Department had been more progressive, presumably it would have taken over the Smith & Wesson production regardless of its patent, licensed it to other manufacturers, and distributed it widely to Union servicemen.

The two top-break revolvers fired, with the .38 S&W cartridge with a light load as for Cowboy Action shooting, showed excellent accuracy. The more modern Model 33 Regulation Police revolver fired with a full power cartridge showed a higher speed, but only a moderate power, 150 foot pounds, not much greater than the Model 2 .32 Army. Again this is a point in favor of the Model 2's effectiveness in the Civil War.

The U.S. Service Model 1917 showed high speed and power and excellent accuracy, consistent with the revolver's popularity in World War I.

The same cartridge was used for shooting the Model 25-2 .45 ACP automatic with a telescopic sight, illustrating the continued popularity of this cartridge. The telescopic sight, producing excellent accuracy, would be used for long range target shooting or hunting.

The .38 Special revolver fired, the Model 36 Chiefs Special, showed surprising accuracy, with its short barrel. The cartridge is clearly substantially more powerful than the earlier .38 S&W.

The firing of the Model 340 AirLiteTiSc revolver demonstrates the advance made by Smith & Wesson's .357 Magnum cartridge. The muzzle velocity and the power are above all the other revolvers fired except for the .44 Magnum, and the accuracy was found to be good, even with the revolver's short 2in barrel. The revolver is surprisingly comfortable to shoot, without the feeling of excessive recoil.

As would be expected, the muzzle velocity and power of the .44 Magnum is substantially above the other revolvers fired. The noise and recoil were also substantial, but the accuracy was found to be surprisingly good even though the shooter would be expected to flinch. There was some impression of a lighter recoil with the ported barrel (a slot near the muzzle slanted forward, allowing the escape of some of the gases). Again, the telescopic sight, which provides a clear picture of the target, is used for long range target shooting and hunting.

Above: Model 33 Regulation Police.

Above: .44 Magnum, ported.

Above: .44 Magnum, with telescopic sight.

BIBLIOGRAPHY

BOOKS

Barnes, Frank C., *Cartridges of The World* (Iola, WI: DBI Books, 1998).

Boorman, Dean K., *The History of Colt Firearms* (New York, NY: Lyons Press, 2001, and Salamander Books, London). *The History of Winchester Firearms* (New York, NY: Lyons Press, 2001, and Salamander Books, London).

Encyclopedia Britannica (Chicago, IL: Enclycopedia Britannica, Inc., 1979).

Flayderman, Norm, *Flayderman's Guide To Antique American Firearms And Their Values*, 8th Edition (Iola, WI: Krause Publications, 2001).

Hogg, Ian V., and Weeks, John S., *Military Small Arms of the 20th Century*, 7th Edition (Iola, WI: Krause Publications, 2000).

Jinks, Roy G., *Artistry In Arms, The Guns of Smith & Wesson* (Springfield, MA: Connecticut Valley Historical Museum, 1991).
History of Smith & Wesson (North Hollywood, CA: Beinfeld Publishing, Inc., 1977).

Keith, Elmer, *Sixguns By Keith* (New York: Bonanza Books, 1961).

Leckie, Robert, *The Wars of America* (New York, NY: Harper and Row, 1981).

Long, Duncan, *Smith & Wesson Autos* (El Dorado, AR: Desert Publications, 1993).

Mullin, Timothy J., *The 100 Greatest Combat Pistols* (Boulder, CO: Paladin Press, 1994).

Smith, Merritt Roe, *Harper's Ferry Armory And The New Technology* (Ithaca, NY: Cornell University Press, 1977).

Supica, Jim, and Nahas, Richard, *Standard Catalog of Smith & Wesson*, Second Edition (Iola, WI: Krause Publications, 2001).

Wallack, L. R., *American Pistol & Revolver Design and Performance* (Tulsa, OK: Winchester Press, 1978).

Walter, John, *The Guns That Won The West* (London: Greenhill Books, 1999).

Wilson, R. L., *Colt, An American Legend* (New York, NY: Abbeville Press, 1955).

PERIODICALS

American Rifleman, National Rifle Association, 11250 Waples Mill Road, Fairfax, VA, 22030.

Guns & Ammo, Primedia Group, PO Box 58505, Boulder CO, 80322.

Man At Arms*, Andrew Mowbray, Inc., PO Box 460, Lincoln, RI, 02865.

The Gun Report*, World-Wide Gun Report, Inc., PO Box 38, Aledo, IL, 61231.

Smith & Wesson Handguns (annual) Primedia Publications, PO Box 1790, Peoria, IL, 61656

ARTICLES

Clapp, Wiley, "The State Of Service Sidearms", *American Rifleman*, May, 2001.

Clapp, Wiley, "Three Of A Kind (Para-Ordnance)", *Guns & Ammo*, May, 2002.

DeRose, Peter, "Smith & Wesson Collectors' Association", *Smith & Wesson Handguns*, 2002.

James, Garry, "Smith & Wesson Goes To War", *Smith & Wesson Handguns*, 2002.

Metcalf, Dick, "S&W Pioneers Handgun Hunting", *Smith & Wesson Handguns*, 2002.

Petty, Charles E., "Inside The New Smith & Wesson", *Guns Magazine*, October, 1994.

Scarlata, Paul, "The Smith & Wesson Military & Police Revolver: Quality Never Becomes Obsolete", *Smith & Wesson Handguns*, 2002.

Wilson, Jim, "The First Magnum", *Smith & Wesson Handguns*, 2002.

* Includes listings of collectors' gun shows.

INDEX